HEIRLOOM QUILTS

By The Staff of WORKBASKET Magazine

KC PUBLISHING, INC.

700 West 47th Street, Suite 310 • Kansas City, Missouri 64112

COPYRIGHT 1995 KC PUBLISHING, INC.

Instructions have been carefully checked for accuracy. The publisher, however, cannot be responsible for human error, misinterpretation of directions or the difference in individual quilters.

ATTENTION: SCHOOLS AND BUSINESS FIRMS
KC Publishing books are available at quantity discounts for bulk purchases for educational, business or sales promotional use. Call Judy Dawson at (816) 531-5730.

LIBRARY OF CONGRESS CATALOGING IN PUBLICATION DATA PENDING.

Printed in Canada

ISBN: 0-86675-346-X

TABLE OF CONTENTS

EDITOR'S FOREWORD

When I grew up, pediatricians had no immunization series to prevent what were labeled "childhood" diseases. Those were the days before daycare or preschool, so wholesale exposure to germs usually didn't begin until kindergarten. So, I suffered the childhood "Big Three" (measles, mumps and chicken pox) all during the first grade. Except to recover enough to go back to school and catch the next "disease du jour," I spent most of the time between Christmas and Easter of 1954-55 in bed.

In those days most every house had a television but not a set in every room. In other words, kids confined to bed had to amuse themselves with books, puzzles and imagination. Lucky for me I also had a handmade quilt. What's so amusing about a quilt? My great-grandmother had made it for me and I loved to follow the intricate designs she had made from scraps of fabric. Those bits of material were very familiar to me. In fact, one of my sick-day games was to try to name their origins. "This was Aunt Sarah's apron; that was Uncle Ed's shirt; my dress last year was made of this..." so my solo narrative would go. Not as exciting as video games or cable television with a remote, but it passed the time. It also made me feel a part of the larger family unit — I belonged and had a secure place in the wide world. Just think, all of that from scraps of fabric stitched together by a old woman's hands!

Quilts are not simply a thrifty bed covering. Quilting itself is an art form and the resulting quilt — made up largely of otherwise unusable bits of material — is an heirloom to be treasured and passed from one generation to another. My great-grandmother is long gone but I still have part of her in that quilt.

In this book we have gathered quilts from far and wide; heirlooms from other grandmothers and great-aunts and cousins and friends from the far corners of the world. These are all honest-to-goodness heirloom quilts made by hand with fingers that were old and weathered by hard work and sometimes crippled with painful arthritis. Yet the results are all beautiful artistic expressions in the form of warmth and function.

We have studied these quilts, researched their origins and put together step-by-step instructions for you to make every one of them yourself. You will find exact dimensions for each quilt pictured, but do not feel limited to making an exact reproduction. If a full-size quilt is more than you can handle, make a mini-version for a wall hanging or a doll quilt. If a small quilt isn't what you want for a king-size bed, by all means make it larger. You will easily be able to make changes and adaptations to any of these traditional patterns and create your very own heirloom quilt.

A collection of quilts with the variety of the one we've gathered here cannot be credited to the efforts of a single person. This book is every bit as much of a collective effort as the old-fashioned quilting bee of days gone by. Special thanks go to Inger Skaarup and Sarah Tobaben Johnson who helped to collect and photograph the quilts; Kim Sawalich who painstakingly put together the pattern directions for each quilt block; and James P. Sexton who prepared all of the technical drawings and full-size pattern templates. Acknowledgment and thanks are also extended to those kind people who helped us find some of the more unusual and obscure quilts and provided picturesque locations to photograph them, including: Rosemary Helms, owner of The Cotton Patch quilt store, the Eureka! Quilters Guild and the Dairy Hollow House bed and breakfast inn, all of Eureka Springs, Arkansas; Jack and Chris Cady of the Pelze-Nichol Haus in Hermann, Missouri; and Jane Overesch of Kansas City, Missouri.

I would also like to add my personal gratitude to Mary Louise St. George Moreau — the great-grandmother who made a quilt for a little girl who has never stopped loving them and those who stitch them.

Kay M. Olson

Kay Melchisedech Olson
Executive Editor

QUILTING BASICS

FABRIC

Color Choices

At the first glance of a finished quilt, we seldom consider the careful pre-planning involved in its successful completion. A common misconception is that a wonderful quilted creation is the result of lucky accident. Any experienced quilter, however, will assure you that success is by design, not chance. Fabric preplanning is a necessary strategy.

To better understand color relationships, it is helpful to consult an artist's color wheel. One of these tools can be obtained from an art supply store or found in a book on design fundamentals. Your local library undoubtedly has such books containing other helpful information regarding color relationships.

For example, colors directly across from each other on the color wheel are known as *contrasting colors*. As the name suggests, the use of contrasting colors can create dynamic results. The traditional Christmas colors of green and red are a classic example of contrasting colors.

A simpler, yet satisfactory, method of color selection is to choose a large print fabric that appeals to your color preferences. Use the colors in this fabric to compare and select your other choices. Pick out colors from its design and look for fabrics that use those colors in different ways. By employing this method of color selection, you can be sure that your fabrics will coordinate nicely.

Be sure to vary the size and types of prints that you select. Random prints are the easiest to work with; stripes, plaids, checks and prints with patterns can sometimes produce awkward results when blocks are assembled. Such choices are most successfully used in borders and large areas, especially for a novice quilter.

Don't forget that solid space is an important design element in designing most quilt blocks. Solid pieces create the strong positive and negative spaces necessary to form and enhance the overall pattern created by the joined pieces.

Finally, consider the tones and values of the various fabrics. The play of light against dark can be the most dramatic effect you use in your quilt. Also realize that swatches of medium tones, though different in color, may blend together when placed side by side. The eye may automatically perceive them as one fabric, thereby defusing the impact of the pattern.

Be very aware of your color and fabric design choices. Pay close attention to how the fabrics will fit together and affect each other. It is wise to make up several sample quilt blocks to ensure ultimate satisfaction with the finished product.

The successful quilter views quilt-making as a pleasurable leisure activity that lends itself to endless creative expression. An enjoyable activity, by its very nature, is one to which you will obviously devote the time necessary to be successful.

When quilting, difficulties that result from poor fabric selection or poor equipment choices will surely put a damper on the enjoyment, which will likewise stifle rather than encourage creativity.

We have prepared many suggestions that are sure to assist you in making sound choices selecting materials that will not only make your work easier but also will allow you to create quilts of heirloom quality and enduring beauty.

Fiber Content and Fabric Preparation

Most quilters prefer 100% cotton fabric, though cotton/polyester blends are rapidly gaining popularity. Whatever you choose, be sure that the fabrics are of consistent weights and fabric content. Puckering and irregular wearing problems will result from inattention to this advice. Consistency of fabric types helps a quilt age gracefully. Also keep in mind that some polyester blends, being tightly woven, may make the actual quilting process more difficult.

Advance preparation of the fabric is another important basic to quilting. Fabric should be washed, dried and pressed before being cut and pieced. Prewashing will set the fabric's color as well as preshrink it, removing any sizing that could restrict your needle movement.

During the laundering of dark or bright colored fabrics, be sure to look in on the rinse cycle. Here you will see if the fabric has a tendency to "bleed" dye. If you discover such a problem, there are several ways to handle the situation.

One popular method to stabilize a fabric's color is to fill the washing machine, set at the low level, with cold water. Add 1-1/4 cups white vinegar and 1/2 cup salt; then soak the fabric in this solution for 4 to 8 hours. Afterward, allow the fabric to finish the wash cycle, noting the color of the rinse water. If the fabric still bleeds, do not use it for the quilt.

Another color stabilization technique is washing the fabric two or three times, checking each rinse cycle to see if the running eventually stops.

Some quilters will go ahead and use fabric that continues to release dye in the wash water, but they know the quilt must be considered "dry clean only." Since quilts are meant to be used, however, most people simply prefer to avoid using fabrics that will destroy the beauty of the overall project when it is cleaned.

Pressing, though often overlooked, is the final step of fabric preparation. Pressing the pre-washed fabric is important to the accuracy of pattern-cutting. The slightest wrinkle can result in an incorrectly cut piece that can, in turn, throw a whole quilt block off measurement. This type of inaccuracy can haunt you throughout the quilt-making process, forcing painful readjustments at practically every turn.

Estimating Yardage

To estimate the amount of fabric you will need for your project, it is helpful to prepare a cutting layout plan. Specifying yardage for each quilt pattern in this collection would limit you to making it in only one size. You may want to make a full-size quilt from a lap-size coverlet, for instance, or scale a king-size quilt down to a doll-size pattern. You will be able to use more flexibility and creativity in making quilts if you are adept at estimating yardage yourself.

The layout can be as simple as a freehand sketch, depending on your drawing skills. Many quilters, however, find it helpful to use graph paper for this step. You can draw your layout using one square to represent an inch or you may want each square to represent 2 inches or more. This preference is entirely up to you, but be sure to write the scale you choose on the graph paper so your measuring remains constant. Realize that you will need a layout for each fabric you use; label each piece as you draw it. Allow for shrinkage and selvage removal in your estimate by subtracting at least 2 inches from the dimensions of the fabric.

Lay out the borders and sashes first, because they are the longest and are best cut from whole pieces of fabric. Add 1/4-inch seam allowances to the sides and an extra 2 inches to lengths for insurance. Also lay out any bindings you want cut from the same materials that are to be used for other pieces. If the binding is *straight grained*, plan for the proper width and length as you did for the borders, but add 6 inches extra to allow for mitered corners. If it is a bias binding, figure that a square yard of fabric yields approximately 16 yards of 2-inch binding.

After the larger pieces have been positioned, smaller pieces can be placed. These pieces may be drawn individually or you can figure how many "like" pieces fit in a 1-foot square. Then deal with these larger "blocks" of fabric.

The total yardage for a full-size quilt is approximately 10 yards. If you carefully consider these generalities, you will likely have as much material as you need, with a little extra. Some quilters prefer to estimate quickly, figuring 1/2 to 1 yard for accent fabrics and 3 yards for each of every other fabric.

The method you chose to figure yardage really depends on your experience level and whether you prefer to save time in estimating yardage (and risk purchasing too much fabric) or save money (by figuring more precisely your exact fabric needs). In either case, it is always better to have a little too much fabric than not enough to complete your quilt.

Beginning the Process

Making Templates

The templates may be made from cardboard, pressboard or artboard, although transparent vinyl (plastic) is the most durable template material. Vinyl pieces can be used many times without wearing down, while the cardboard-type products may be slowly shaved away by the frequent passes of pencils, cutters or scissors.

The patterns in this book are given with the 1/4-inch seam allowances included. When making templates, some quilt makers like to mark the exact seam lines on the fabric pieces. If this is the case, you may want to make a template that has been cut on the seam line (broken lines) *in addition to* the template with seam allowances. After the piece has been cut from the full template, the seam line template can be laid on top of the fabric piece and the exact seam lines drawn.

A more straightforward approach is to make a window template, which allows for both cutting and seam line to be drawn at the same time. Double check this type of template before use, however, to be sure both sets of measurements are accurate.

If you are using cardboard, pressboard, artboard, or an opaque plastic for your templates, first trace the pattern pieces with tissue paper. Then glue the tissue paper to the template material and cut out the pieces with scissors. Before cutting the pieces, be sure to use a straight edge to check for accuracy and minimize distortion.

When using a clear vinyl template, place the vinyl over the printed pattern, tracing directly onto the vinyl. Cut out the pieces, labeling each as you go. Again, use a straight edge whenever possible to ensure precise lines.

When labeling the pieces, be sure to identify the name of the quilt block, and any piece number or letter indicated on the pattern drawing. You may also want to mark any indicated grain lines and the number of pieces needed. Above all, take the time to make a sample block to test the accuracy of your template pieces before cutting the pieces for the entire quilt.

Cutting Pieces From Fabric

Having properly prepared the fabric, cut the selvage edges from each piece. Then, choose your cutting instrument and continue accordingly.

When cutting with *dressmaker's shears*, the fabric can be folded and pinned or layered double and pinned. Cutting more than two layers with shears can result in some distortion of bottom layers. However, in preparation for *rotary cutting*, as many as six pieces of fabric can be layered and cut simultaneously.

In either case, be sure to align the grain of each fabric layer and hold the cutting blades as straight up and down as possible so that all pieces are identical.

With the layers of fabric spread in front of you, wrong side up, place the templates face down on the fabric and trace them carefully with your marker. For appliqué techniques, you may prefer to have the fabric right side up so the cut lines and seam lines are marked on the right side of the fabric. In this case, be sure to also put the templates

face up. After marking pattern pieces, double check the accuracy of lines drawn before cutting with shears or using a straight edge to cut the lines with a rotary cutter.

Once cutting is completed, most quilt makers prefer to press all seam allowances. Also, bundling and counting identical pieces should be done now; thread a needle with contrasting thread and knot the end. Then insert the needle consecutively through the center of the pieces to "stack" them. Simply pull the thread snugly and knot it on top of the stack. You can never be too organized, when dealing with several hundred small quilt block pieces.

Assembling the Quilt Top

The decision to hand piece or machine piece is purely a personal one. There are many variables to consider. While hand piecing is portable and considered quite relaxing, machine piecing is faster and produces stronger results. The soft lines of a hand stitched quilt are generally judged the most aesthetically pleasing. Some quilters strike a happy compromise by hand stitching the quilt blocks and machine stitching the borders, sashing and bindings. Such a compromise provides the positive benefits of both types of quilt assembly.

Whether you choose to hand stitch or machine stitch your quilt, keep in mind that the accuracy of your stitching is imperative to successful results. Any mistakes are best corrected as they occur; later adjustments may be more complicated than you might imagine.

The Pieced Block

In the piecing process, the initial step is to create the quilt blocks; the pattern chosen will determine exactly where you will start. First, lay out the pieces of a block to get a mental picture of the correct placement. It is best to assemble the pieces in rows, if possible, since straight seams are easier to piece than seams that must turn corners. However, some quilt patterns, such as a star block, begin assembly from the center of the design. Keep this advice in mind when planning your procedure, and follow the appropriate directions.

Hand Stitching

When hand stitching, hold two pieces together, with right sides facing. Pin the corners of the two pieces, inserting the pin at the points (indicated by black dots) where stitching lines meet. Then pin the rest of the joining seam. Next, sew the pieces along the seam line, using short running stitches, with eight to 10 stitches per inch. Backstitch both at the beginning and the end to secure the seam; be sure to begin and end your stitching at the points where seams converge and *do not stitch down seam allowances*. In this way, the allowances will remain free, making it easier to sew intersecting seams and press them in different directions when necessary.

As rows of joined blocks are attached, situations will arise where you must intersect a previously sewn seam. In such a case, sew up to the seam allowance (the seam line point of the piece) and make a backstitch to lock. Then, pass the needle through the seam points, backstitching once on the other side and continuing the seam from there. Once again, avoid sewing down the seam allowance.

Machine Stitching

The process for machine stitching is slightly different than the hand stitching method. Be sure to keep the 1/4-inch seam allowances accurate, and the stitch length around 12 stitches per inch. Measure from the needle to the 1/4-inch mark on the face plate. If the measurement is not accurate, try to adjust the position of your needle. If you are unable to adjust the needle, determine the correct placement for a 1/4-inch mark and put down a piece of masking tape to serve as a guide.

It isn't easy to sew from seam line to seam line on the sewing machine so it is common practice to simply sew the pieces completely across the seam allowance. Therefore, you must plan ahead to fold seam allowances toward the darker fabric, when possible. Or, when joining two rows of pieced blocks, turn intersecting seam allowances toward opposite sides to avoid fabric bulk. In this procedure, it is best to turn the seam allowance on the bottom toward the back of the machine and the top seam allowance toward you. Experiment with your sewing machine to find the way easiest for you to control the stitching.

Do not open seams, as is common with garment sewing, however. The quilt needs the added strength provided by folded over seams. Open seams leave the stitches more vulnerable and exposed to wear, while a seam that is turned to one side backs the stitches with a layer of cloth.

An experienced machine quilter may use a technique called chain stitching. For this process you must have many "like" pieces ready to be joined. The pieces are fed through the machine, one after another, allowing the machine to make a few stitches between pieces with nothing under the needle. These sewing threads "chain" the pieces together to aid in organization. The pieces can be separated at a later time, as needed.

Meeting Multiple Points

When matching multiple points, at the center of a star block, for instance, begin by marking all seam line corners on the individual pieces. Sew sections together in pairs, being sure to stop and start all stitches *on the corner dot*. Backstitch at this point to lock. Locking is necessary whether you are hand stitching or machine stitching because there will be no crossing seam. Connect pairs to pairs, and so on, until the star is complete. Working in this manner will help you stay in control.

Appliqué

The pieces of a hand appliqué quilt are sewn to a whole piece of fabric called a foundation block. Once cut, the small pieces are laid face down on an ironing board and the 1/4-inch seam allowances are pressed back. Clip seam allowances to ease curves and trim excess fabric, if necessary, when folding in corners. Next, pin and baste the pieces to the foundation block according to the placement guide. You may wish to fold and press the foundation block to temporarily mark the center as an aid in the placement of appliqué pieces. Layer the pieces from the background of the block forward, keeping in mind that edges layered under other pieces don't need to be turned under. Finish the appliqué with a blind, or hemming, stitch. Use thread that matches the appliqué rather than the foundation block and take small stitches to keep the stitches as invisible as possible. Finally, cut away the portion of the foundation block that is beneath the appliqué, leaving a 1/4-inch seam allowance around the edges.

Freezer paper is often used in place of basting, when applying an appliqué. Pattern pieces are cut from the freezer paper, with the 1/4-inch seam allowances removed. The fabric piece is then placed face down on the ironing board and the freezer paper is centered and pinned between the stitching lines, shiny side up. The 1/4-inch seam allowance of the fabric piece is then folded over and lightly touched with the tip of the iron, fusing it back. Finally, the appliqué is fused in like manner to the foundation block. The freezer paper may be removed after the portion of the foundation block behind the appliqué has been cut away.

To machine appliqué the pieces, you will need to trim off the 1/4" seam allowances and fuse the pieces to the foundation block using a lightweight fusible web, available at most fabric stores. Or you may stabilize the appliqué piece with iron-on fusible interfacing and machine baste it to the block. The edges of the appliqué piece are covered using the machine's satin stitch. The stitching should be applied evenly and completely cover the raw edges. It is best to use a stitch wide enough to cover the appliqué's raw edge and still cover a small amount of fabric on each side. In this manner you will ensure that the appliqué will stay attached and won't ravel.

When using the sewing machine to appliqué, plan to clean built-up lint, oil the machine and replace dull needles often. You may also find it helpful to wind several bobbins with thread before you begin.

Press and Check

Press each block carefully, being sure that seams lay evenly to avoid any bunched seams showing through. Seams should be pressed toward the darker piece, making allowances less visible from the front side. Correct problems in blocks by removing a few stitches and easing puckered areas, then resew. Check to see that all blocks are square; correct any irregularities at this point.

Setting the Quilt Top

Before you begin to set or sew together the blocks, lay them out along with any stripping or other pieces on a large surface. This procedure allows you to check the fit and observe the visual effect the final arrangement will have. The placement will often be altered at this point because the finished product is more apparent than it has been so far. At this point, corrections and adjustments to the latticework and borders can also be made.

A diagonally-set quilt will have half square triangles and quarter square triangles filling the edges and corners, creating the rectangular shape. Sometimes a pattern will call for the cutting of completed squares to fill these gaps, while others use plain fabric.

When cutting these triangles from plain cloth, it is best to cut them with the grain of the fabric running along what will be the outside edge of the pieced rectangle. Such a quilt will be sturdy and easier to bind. Here a bias edge would have more stretch and would be harder to control when finishing.

Once you are satisfied with the arrangement of the quilt top, begin stitching the blocks together by rows. Pin corners first, followed by the seams, then stitch with short running stitches. Join finished rows two at a time, matching vertical seams before sewing. Next, join these sections until the top is complete. Finally, trim any excess material or threads from the backside and press both front and back. Take care to turn seam allowances to the side least visible from the front and create the least bulk.

Borders

Borders, along with sashing or latticework, are the "framework" of many quilts. They enlarge dimensions, add design options, and enhance the overall beauty of a quilt. Borders are generally either mitered or blunt. Mitered bor-

ders are effective when the fabric has a directional print. They create a formal "picture frame" appearance, appropriate for wall display. Blunt, often called Amish, borders are quite easy to master and can also be visually pleasing.

Before adding the border, be sure to take this opportunity to measure the previously assembled quilt center. The center, made up of any blocks and sashing, should be measured to be sure that the measurements of corresponding sides are true. The measurement across the top should equal the measurement across the bottom, as should random measurements across various areas of the middle. Likewise, the vertical measurement of each side should be identical, as should the vertical measurement at the center. Make any necessary adjustments at this time.

Matching the quilt's center points, pin the border to the patchwork piece. Sew according to the following directions, with 1/4-inch seams.

Mitered Borders

If you have planned multiple mitered borders, it is best to attach all borders at once. Simply sew all corresponding strips together, forming a large solid border for each side. This procedure will allow you to miter the corners simultaneously, with one continuous seam at each corner.

For machine stitching, begin and end the border seams at the seam line point. Attach all four borders, leaving the corners overlapping and loose. Lay a protractor or straight edge across the loose ends, from corner to corner and mark a diagonal line. Repeat for all four strips at both ends of each border. These markings are the seam lines for the mitered corners. Simply fold the quilt diagonally, from each corner, and stitch the seam. Trim the excess fabric, leaving a 1/4-inch seam allowance.

If hand stitching, attach the borders, stopping at seam line points to leave corners loose. Cut the strips flush on the outside edge to form square corners. Turn back one of the strips from the center to form a mitered seam, and blind stitch. Repeat this process for each of the four corners.

Blunt (Amish) Borders

First, apply the top and bottom borders, stitching the borders completely across. Then attach the side border strips, folding under the 1/4-inch seam allowance where the top strip crosses the bottom strip. Blind stitch this seam. Trim the ends of the borders, leaving the corners square. To apply multiple Amish borders, it is best to attach one border at a time, creating a stair-step appearance.

THE QUILTING PROCESS

Marking Quilt Top Patterns

Before assembling the layers, you must consider what design the quilt stitches will follow.

No marking is necessary if the quilting will follow along the seam lines of patchwork or appliqués. Generally, outline quilting runs 1/4-inch from the seams surrounding patches, though many quilters prefer to "quilt in-the-ditch," or right next to the seam opposite the pressed seam allowance. A very similar technique is echo quilting, in which the contour of an appliqué or motif is repeated many times with stitch lines.

These methods are common in pieced or appliquéed quilts, where this is often enough quilting to hold everything securely together.

Quilts with large open areas or plain borders often require more stitching; a decorative pattern is often employed. These designs must be marked on the quilt top before further assembly. Patterns can be marked using stencils, available at quilt shops and some fabric stores, or with homemade templates. Simply place the stencil on the quilt top and mark with your choice of soluble marker (be sure to test solubility *on a test piece of your fabric* before using). You may find a pattern you like in a book, in which case you can photocopy the design, then tape it to a windowpane and hold the fabric over it to trace. This method works well on medium- to light-colored fabrics. When stitching a straight line, masking tape can be used as a guide that is easily removed. Be sure to leave masking tape in place for *only a short time*, because adhesive may adhere to the fabric if left in place long. Also, avoid ironing over areas marked with pencil or markers, because heat makes some marking permanent.

Special Effects

A quilt requiring techniques such as Trapunto, English padding or stuffed appliqué will need these embellishments applied before the layering begins. Involving cording or stuffing between stitched fabric layers, these techniques add a sculpted quality by raising the design in chosen areas.

Lining (or Quilt Back)

Preparation of the quilt backing will vary according to your fabric choice. There are several options, however, some guidelines should be followed to get quality results.

When using a bed sheet for the lining, measure to be sure that the length and width are sufficient to back the quilt top with two to four inches to spare on all sides. Also be sure that the lengthwise grain runs the length of the quilt; this direction may not be apparent if the hems and finished edges have been removed.

You may find a suitable fabric that is wide enough for your lining from a bolt. However, you will probably need to piece the backing. In this case, run a full width of the fabric down the center length of the quilt, adding strips to each side that are wide enough to complete the lining, plus two to four extra inches all around. This placement is preferred because the two vertical seams add strength and will be less noticeable than a center seam, if there is any show-through or bulkiness. Unlike seams joining pieces in the quilt blocks, backing seams should be pressed open, being sure the material is smooth and ready for layering.

Layering and Basting

Spread the prepared backing on a large, flat surface with the right side down. Next, place the filler on top of the lining, being careful not to stretch or distort the batting while positioning. Batting is available in large sizes, but if piecing is necessary, slightly overlap and baste. Place the quilt top over the filler, right side up. Check the squareness of the layers, being sure that there was no shifting and the grains are all in alignment. Accuracy here is essential for a smooth, symmetrical quilt.

Pin and baste the three layers together. Pin the layers at the center and the corners, then in several other places, to prevent shifting while stitching. Baste with large stitches, using a contrasting thread to simplify removal after the quilting process. Basted seams should run from corner to corner and horizontally and vertically through the center. A seam also runs approximately 6 inches from the edge, along each side, with additional vertical and horizontal seams added as needed. Seams should be evenly spaced to securely anchor all layers.

Some quilters find basting stitches difficult to remove after machine quilting, so they prefer to "baste" the entire quilt with large safety pins. This method will take several dozen pins to adequately hold the entire quilt; be sure to have enough on hand. Be careful to remove pins before machine stitching over them, to avoid breaking a needle.

Quilt Stitching

Hand Quilting

Once you have mounted the quilt on a quilting frame or hoop, you are ready to begin quilting. If you are a novice,

9

you may want to use white or off-white thread, as it tends to reveal fewer imperfections than does thread of a contrasting color. Thread a quilting needle with 20 inches of thread and put your thimble on the middle finger of your working hand; place your free hand under the stitching area and your working hand on top. Insert the needle about an inch from where you want stitching to begin. Bring the needle through the top, then the batting, and the top again. This stitch comes up where you want to begin quilting.

While holding the material firmly, pull gently on the thread until the knot pops through the top and into the batting. This method will anchor the thread so you can begin quilting. Keep stitches straight and even, pushing the needle with the thimble on your middle finger while guiding the fabric with the thumb on the same hand and your index finger on the hand beneath. Be careful to keep the stitches tight enough to hold the layers securely, but not so tight that the fabric puckers.

Stop stitching when you are down to about 5 inches of thread on the needle. Then, either take a short backstitch or knot the thread close (but not snug) to the fabric, to lock the stitching. *DO NOT CUT THREAD.*

Finish with a long stitch through the quilt top, batting and quilt top (as in the beginning); pull gently to pop the knot into the batting and trim thread even with material. If you chose a backstitch to lock the thread, you will still want to take this last stitch to "bury" the end of the thread inside the layers; simply omit the pulling of the knot.

To make sure these ends stay buried, some quilters apply a small drop of fabric glue to the knot and/or thread end before making the long stitch. When the glue dries, the thread is secured to the batting inside.

Machine Quilting

Be well-acquainted with your machine's capabilities before beginning machine quilting. If you have a newer, more advanced machine, it may have particular attachments or settings that are specifically designed for quilting. If not, you may want check to see if you can obtain an even feed attachment for your machine model. Experimentation may be necessary if there aren't sufficient directions in your machine's user's manual.

The sample quilt block you made earlier will be handy here. Simply cut a piece each of backing and batting; then, layer and baste. This block will help you determine appropriate settings, because it is similar to the quilt you will be stitching.

Use invisible thread, for the top thread, so you will be able to sew over all fabrics without stopping to change thread color. Use a cotton/polyester thread in the bobbin to

match the lining material. Set the machine at eight to 10 stitches per inch and test stitch to see if you need to adjust the tension. Consult the machine's manual if you aren't familiar with this adjustment.

When quilting by machine, fold and roll the quilt into a manageable size. It is best to roll in from both sides, then fold up from the bottom. Begin the stitching in the center area. Plan to sew as straight a pattern as possible, because turning may cause pulling.

Be aware that small tucks are inevitable where sewing lines cross. Most machine quilters simply overlook this imperfection, unless the tuck is just too big to be missed. In such a case, remove the stitches in the offending area and resew. After all vertical lines are stitched, roll and fold from the top and bottom to sew horizontal lines.

If you don't mind rerolling and folding, you may be able to take a different approach. Sew one vertical seam down the center, then reroll to sew any horizontal seams that intersect it, in the center. Continue back and forth this way, from the center outward. Although this method takes a little more effort in folding, it will likely result in a quilt with more even appearance, with less tucking on the back side.

Tied Quilt

If the quilt is thick it may be difficult or impossible to quilt. In such a case, it would be best to tie the quilt every 3 to 6 inches. First, mark the quilt top with fabric marker for desired placement, being sure these tie points are evenly spaced.

Insert a large-eyed darning needle, threaded with heavy thread or yarn, through all layers at tie points. Leaving about 1/4-inch space, bring the needle back up through the quilt. Finally, with at least a 2-inch length on both sides, cut the thread and tie it in a tight square knot. If desired, the knot can be made even more secure by stitching over it with a sewing machine's zig-zag stitch. This procedure is called making a *bar tack*.

BINDING THE QUILT

The final stage in the quilting process is binding the quilt edges. There are many methods from which to choose.

One simple method is to trim the backing material so it is approximately 1-1/4 inches shorter than the quilt top on all sides. Turn under 1/4 inch of the top and fold it over the backing 1 inch, blind stitching it in place to form a hem line.

You can also do the reverse by trimming the backing so that it exceeds the measurement of the top by 1-1/4 inches, bringing the backing over the top and hem stitching in the same manner. Provided the fabric chosen for backing is a coordinating one, this choice is an easy one. For neat corners, fold the point over first, then the corresponding edges, to form a mitered seam.

The most common procedure is to add a long, continuous strip of fabric, blind stitching it to both the top and bottom layer. First, trim the three layers evenly all around. Then whip stitch around the edges to hold them securely. Finally, attach the binding.

To find the length of binding needed, measure the distance around the quilt, adding 12 inches allowance. Then cut strips, about 2-1/2-inches wide, from the chosen fabric. If possible, a more durable fabric should be used for binding, or you may want to double the width of the binding, folding it in half before attaching. This binding, referred to as "French binding," gives extra strength to the quilt.

Binding strips may be cut either on the bias or with the grain, according to personal preference. Bias bindings are often preferred simply because they are the traditional choice. They may be best where there is an irregular or curved edge that requires greater flexibility.

The current trend is to cut the binding with the grain for straight edged quilts. Having less stretch, this binding is easier to control. In addition, a binding cut with the grain can take advantage of any directional lines or patterns printed on the fabric. Conversely, a bias binding can obscure such a pattern, if that is the desired effect.

Whichever style binding you choose, a rotary cutter, mat and quilter's ruler will be of great service in cutting the necessary strips. If you are piecing the binding, be sure to join strips with diagonal seams to reduce bulkiness where it is folded and sewn. Simply cut the ends of the strips at a 45° angle and join with a seam.

Continuous Binding - Mitered Corners

When attaching a continuous binding, begin in the middle of a side to assure that all corners will be identical. With the back of the quilt upward, pin the binding along the edge, with right side facing the quilt. Sew a 1/4-inch seam to attach the binding. At the corners, stop 1/4 inch before the end of the edge, backstitching to lock and cut thread.

Turn the quilt and binding, folding the binding strip over itself, creating a 45° fold. Place the binding edge along the next quilt edge and pin. Stitch the 1/4-inch seam and continue around in this manner until you meet the beginning of the binding.

Overlap the ends, folding under the raw edge and stitch to join. Fold the binding over to the front, turning 1/4 inch under for a hem. Blind stitch around the front edge and neatly tuck in extra fabric at the corners, blind stitching to finish mitered corners.

Square Corners

Alternately, you may prefer a less complicated method, or want to enhance the "stair-step" effect of an Amish border. In this case, finish each side separately, overlapping the corners for a squared look. As before, sew the binding to the back with a 1/4-inch seam, turning to the front to blind stitch. When employing this method, begin at a corner and apply all four sides separately.

First attach the top and bottom binding strips, whip stitching the open ends to the quilt body. Then attach side binding strips, overlapping at the corners. Remember to extend the raw ends of the side strips 1/2 inch, then fold in the extra fabric and blind stitch as the final step.

French Binding

This binding method is both easy to apply and durable, affording a double layer of material around the perimeter of the quilt. This double layer is beneficial, as this area experiences the greatest amount of stress. As previously mentioned, the strip's width is figured by multiplying the finished width by four, plus two seam allowances. For example: If you want a 1-inch binding, the strips would need to be 4-1/2 inches (4 x 1" +1/4" +1/4"). Fold the strips lengthwise, right side out, and press. The raw edge is then positioned along the raw edge of the quilt on the back side, and stitched with a 1/4-inch seam allowance. The binding is then folded to the front, enclosing the quilt edge and seam allowances, and blind stitched. The corners can be mitered or blunt, and are handled, according to your preference, by following methods mentioned earlier.

Prairie Points

A decorative alternative to binding, called "prairie points," allows you to carry a geometric theme to the edge of the quilt. There are two ways to create this effect. The traditional method allows you to mix fabrics in the binding while the modern technique incorporates strip quilting ideas for quick results. Either method will produce the desired effect.

Traditional Application

Begin by cutting small, uniform squares of fabric; the exact size is your choice. The edges of the squares generally measure from 2 to 4 inches. The sizes of other pieces in the quilt top will help you decide what size prairie points will look best.

You must also decide whether the points will be of the same fabric, or if the binding will reflect the many fabrics of the quilt top. If you choose to assemble the binding from one fabric, you may opt for the quick method, instead.

For the traditional prairie points, fold each square in half diagonally, then iron the crease flat. Fold the resulting triangles in half and press again, forming the "points." Insert the folded edge of a "point" into the open edge of another. Position and pin them in this manner across the edge of the quilt. Next, sew this chain of points to the quilt, then fold them up and fold seam allowances back. Turn under a 1/4-inch seam allowance on the backing and blind stitch to the back of the row of "points."

Quick Method

Begin by preparing strips of fabric. Determine the size of squares you will need and add 1/4 inch to find the width of the strips. The length will be determined by measuring each quilt edge, adding approximately 6 inches for allowance. These strips may be pieced if necessary.

Make perpendicular cuts in the strip, leaving 1/4 inch uncut along the bottom edge of the strip. These cuts will be made at intervals equal to the measurement you determined for the square size. Fold each square in half diagonally. Fold again in the other direction and press. As with the traditional method, the points are sewn to the quilt top layer, then turned up. The backing is turned under and blind stitched to the back of the prairie points.

With either method, the folds in the individual "points" can be adjusted to help fit the dimensions of the quilt. If a strip is about an inch too long or short, simply adjust several folds a little. Over the span of 10 or 12 points, an inch can be easily adjusted. End triangles of each strip may also be folded one additional time, giving edges a squared-off look.

LABELING THE QUILT

As with any piece of artwork, the artist needs to sign the masterpiece. Today, much time is devoted to researching the origins of quilts sewn hundreds of years ago. Likewise, much energy is spent tracking lost quilts of both historical quilters and family ancestors. This work would be easier had the quilter taken the time to sign and date the work.

Sign your quilt with embroidery, cross stitch, even permanent marker or typewriting on a spare piece of fabric. Then turn the fabric edges under and whip stitch it to a back corner of the quilt.

Your "signature" can include more than your name. Many quilters include the name of the quilt, quilt maker's name, the date, city and state in which it was made, and some special sentiment.

Antique quilts were often signed with the name and date beautifully embroidered into a quilt top motif. This signature technique could be the perfect addition to a treasured memento, so be sure to take the time to preserve memories by labeling your quilt.

Amish borders These are borders that are joined with overlapping, square corners, as opposed to mitered corners.

appliqué A piece of fabric that is cut and sewn to a larger piece, or to a foundation block, using embroidery, blind stitching or satin zigzag machine stitching.

backing The bottom layer of a quilt.

bar tack Method whereby a machine zigzag stitch is used to secure the yarn or thread ties on a tied quilt.

basting The long, loose running stitches that hold together the layers of a quilt and restrict movement during the quilting process.

batting The insulating material used in the middle layer of a quilt.

bias Term referring to the diagonal, or 45° angle, of a woven fabric.

binding A strip of fabric used to enclose the raw edges of the assembled quilt.

block Frequently referred to as a quilt block or square, it is a unit that is designed and joined to other blocks to create the quilt top. Although the name implies a rectangular or square shape, it can be any geometric shape.

border Strips of cloth that create a framework for the quilt top.

calico A cotton fabric on which a pattern is repeated in 1-inch increments.

chain-stitching This technique is performed on a sewing machine. Several pieces are stitched in succession, letting the machine take three or four stitches without fabric under the needle between swatches. This technique helps the quilter move quickly and keeps pieces organized.

comforter An especially thick quilt, often reversible and made of a solid fabric.

coverlet This term generally refers to a quilt or spread that is only large enough to cover the bed top and pillows.

echo quilting Quilt stitching that surrounds an appliqué or shape. This stitching is then repeated an unlimited number of times to resemble an "echo" or outgoing waves.

fabric marker A special pen, tailor's chalk or other writing

COMMON QUILTING TERMS

implement made for marking templates or quilt patterns onto the quilt top. It is a good idea to test the removability of the markings on fabric before using.

filler The middle layer of the quilt. Usually the filler is made up of some sort of batting. This layer gives the quilt its insulating quality. (see batting)

finger-press To press fabric between fingers, forming a slight crease.

foundation block In appliqué quilts, this piece is a solid block of fabric on which smaller pieces of fabric are arranged and sewn.

grain This term refers to the direction that the threads run in the fabric. When instructed to place a pattern "with the grain" or "on the grain" it generally means the lengthwise grain that runs parallel to the fabric's selvage edge. The grain is the direction of greatest strength in the fabric.

grid A pattern of evenly placed horizontal and vertical lines that may be found on a cutting board, mat, or a quilter's ruler. A grid is an aid in measuring and squaring pieces as you cut.

latticework The lengths of fabric used to separate or frame pattern blocks. Also referred to as stripping or sashing.

lining In quilting, this term is often used in reference to the back, or bottom layer of the quilt.

loft This term refers to the thickness of the batting. When purchasing batting, it is sometimes referred to by a numbering system; generally the higher the number, the thicker the batting.

miter To join two intersecting pieces, usually a border or binding, at a corner to form a 45 ° angled seam.

outline quilting To quilt stitch 1/4 inch from seam, around patchwork or appliqué pieces.

pane A term sometimes used to refer to a quilt block.

patch A broad term that can refer to a small piece of fabric or an entire quilt block.

patched quilt Usually refers to an appliquéed quilt.

pieced quilt Usually refers to a quilt in which the top is created from small pieces of fabric sewn together.

pressing To use the weight of a warm steam iron to flatten and smooth the quilt pieces or seams while working.

quilting Refers to the sewing stitches that hold the three layers of a quilt (top, batting and backing) together securely, and can include anything from a single tied stitch to decorative stitching.

quilt top The upper layer of a quilt consisting of a single piece of fabric, joined blocks, appliqués, embroidered fabric or any combination of these; the embellished layer.

rotary cutting Refers to cutting with a rotary cutter (for more information, see supplies information list).

sashes or sashing See latticework.

seam allowance The distance between the stitching line (broken line on patterns) and the cutting line (solid line) of your fabric pieces. In this book, it is 1/4-inch wide.

selvage The bound edge on both sides of a bolt of fabric, which prevents raveling. Remove selvages before pieces are cut because they cause uneven fabric shrinkage.

setting Assembling of all the pieces (blocks, latticework and borders) of the quilt top.

stitch-in-the-ditch To quilt along the edge of a seam on the side opposite the seam allowance.

stripping Refers either directly to the lattice work (or sashing) or the act of applying the strips of latticework.

template A pattern piece cut from cardboard or plastic, used to trace the pieces for the quilt top or to trace the patterns for the quilting stitches.

tied quilt A quilt on which the three layers (top, filler and backing) are fastened together with single knotted stitches that are evenly placed. Recommended mainly for extremely thick quilts.

tie points Marks made with a fabric marker to ensure even placement of "ties" on a tied quilt.

top An abbreviated term referring to the quilt top.

whip stitch A small overcast stitch, sometimes used to prepare the edges of a quilt before binding.

GLOSSARY OF STITCHING TECHNIQUES

backstitch Used primarily as embroidery when signing an American quilt, or when extra strength is needed in a seam. Traditionally used in Europe as a quilting stitch, but replaced by the running type quilting stitch for American quilting.

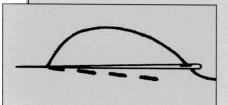

Begin by making one running stitch. Then, insert the needle back to the beginning of the first stitch, bringing it up through the cloth at an equal distance past the first stitch. This an overlapping running stitch that creates a solid, strong line of stitching.

back lock stitch This stitch is used to fasten off the last stitch in a row as an alternative to tying a knot. Simply repeat the last stitch over itself two or more times. When quilt stitching, follow this stitch with a long stitch into the batting, then back up through the top. Cut thread even with quilt top, and let the thread ease back into batting, to bury ends.

basting Typically this term refers to long running stitches, whose function is to temporarily hold fabric and/or batting in place until final stitching is possible. Basting can be done by hand or by machine. For machine basting, lengthen the stitch setting and slightly loosen the tension setting.

Straight pins or safety pins can also be used to baste. When using straight pins, be sure to place heads all in one direction, for easy removal when sewing. If using safety pins, be sure to have several dozen extra large, rust resistant pins.

buttonhole stitch This stitch is often used to secure quilt edges, before binding. It is also a decorative option when attaching appliqués or embellishing strips and blocks in a "crazy quilt". Simply insert needle through fabric then catch thread (as shown) and pull it through. Stitches should be snug, but not excessively tight.

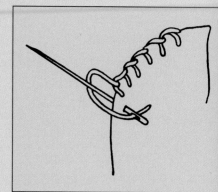

hemming stitch Commonly used wherever a hidden stitch is desired in the joining of two pieces of fabric. It is an appropriate choice for attaching appliqués, mitering corners of borders and bindings, and attaching binding strips.

Begin by bringing the needle up from the underside, through the top fabric (or appliqué). Bring the needle up as close to the seam line as possible, hiding the knot. Insert the needle into the background fabric as close to the first stitch as possible, thus keeping the visible part of the stitch small. Keeping the needle slightly angled, bring it back up through the appliqué. The stitch is then repeated

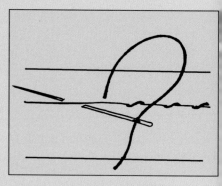

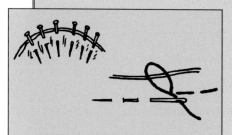

14

*Quilt-making requires the mastery of only a few basic stitch techniques.
If you have any sewing experience, you have undoubtedly encountered most or all of these stitches.
If you are a beginner, however, you may want to practice these simple techniques
on a sample quilt block before attempting them on a full-size quilt.*

as desired, keeping stitches close and even, for more strength.

invisible stitch See hemming stitch.

quilting stitch The function of this stitch is to securely, and permanently, fasten the layers of the quilt in place. Though the quilt stitching serves a vital purpose, it usually takes a quite decorative form. It is generally a short running stitch, with six to ten stitches per inch. It may follow the piecing, patches or ornately marked lines drawn on the quilt top.

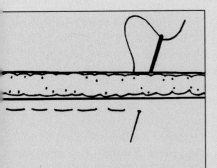

Position yourself with your working hand on top of the quilt, and your other hand beneath. Then insert the needle at a slight angle, through all three layers, with your working hand. Holding the backing and filler up against the top with your free hand, you will feel the needle point come through the bottom. Guide it back up with your free hand and continue working in this manner, "loading" two or three stitches before pulling the needle through.

If the quilt is thicker, or you are a beginner, you may prefer to insert the needle, pulling it through from the bottom. Now, reinsert it from the bottom, spacing the stitch about 1/8 inch, then pull it through from the top. This method will take more time, but if the stitches are more even, it will be worth it.

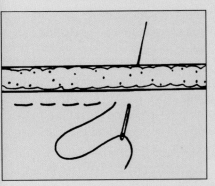

Many sewing machines are capable of quilt stitching. Check your owner's manual or experiment with a test square before trying to machine stitch on your quilt.

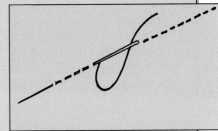

running stitch One of the most used stitches in quilt making, it is basically the same stitch as the quilting stitch and is used to connect patches, blocks, borders, and so forth. Using an in-and-out motion, "load" several small, even stitches on the needle. Then, pull the needle through and tighten stitches.

tie stitch Quilts that are too thick to quilt in the traditional manner may require a hand-tied stitch to secure the layers. Thread a large-eyed yarn needle with a heavy thread, yarn or string. Insert the thread from the top of the quilt, straight through all layers. Leaving about 1/4 inch of space, bring the needle back up through, to the top. Finally, leaving at least 2 inches on both ends, cut the string, pull it snug and tie with a square knot.

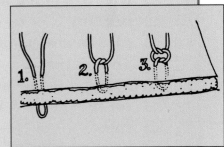

whip stitch A small overcast stitch that is easy and quick to apply; sometimes used to bind quilt edges before binding.

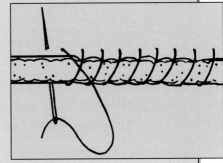

15

What You'll Need

While it's true that the original art of quilting embraced the notion of "making do" with items on hand, there are a few necessary tools of the trade. In addition to the suggested items on the supplies checklist, many contemporary quilters and designers find that access to a photocopy machine or a computer with drawing software can be extremely helpful. You won't necessarily need such high-tech equipment to make your first quilt, but we do suggest you have the following on hand:

SUPPLIES CHECKLIST

- ❏ **backing**
- ❏ **batting**
- ❏ **beeswax**
- ❏ **colored pencils or crayons**
- ❏ **compass**
- ❏ **fabric marker**
- ❏ **iron & ironing board**
- ❏ **needles**
- ❏ **pins & pin cushion**
- ❏ **protractor**
- ❏ **quilting frame or hoop**
- ❏ **rotary cutter & mat**
- ❏ **ruler**
- ❏ **seam ripper**
- ❏ **sewing machine** (optional)
- ❏ **scissors**
- ❏ **shears**
- ❏ **template material**
- ❏ **thimble**
- ❏ **thread**
- ❏ **tissue** (tracing) **paper**
- ❏ **tracing wheel & carbon**

backing — Many quilt makers prefer using 100 percent cotton muslin for the back of the quilt. Others prefer to use decorative calico or the soft warmth of flannel. The modern trend, however, is to take advantage of the many colors and patterns available in bed sheets. This choice has become a viable alternative, offering the convenience of a single piece of cloth. When using a bed sheet to back a quilt, always remove selvages and hems. Regardless of what type of fabric is used for the backing, remember to prewash and dry it before using.

batting — The filler, for the middle layer of the quilt, is generally available in two different fiber contents, both of which are easy to use. Traditional cotton batting is not always easy to find; polyester batting is more readily available. Batting comes in a variety of lofts and sizes. It also comes bonded or unbonded, meaning that the fibers are lightly held in place by a light, undetectable film.

beeswax — Wax is used to make the thread easier to pull through the several layers of a quilt. The simplest method is to hold two cakes in one hand and pull through the threaded length, to coat it lightly.

color pencils or crayons — When planning different color combinations, a box of crayons or colored pencils come in handy. Copy the block patterns on a photocopy machine and experiment with different combinations the way you once filled in the lines of a coloring book.

compass — This tool from geometry class is also useful when designing original blocks, appliqués, or quilt stitch patterns.

computer — When combined with drawing software, a computer can be extremely helpful as a designing tool to create new patterns.

fabric marker — Pencils, water soluble markers or tailors chalk are invaluable when tracing from templates or when marking quilting designs onto the quilt top. Be sure to use water soluble markers so that the markings can be washed away easily.

needles — A packaged assortment of "sharps" is ideal for hand piecing and appliqué. A package of "betweens" in sizes 7 through 12, which are stronger and shorter, are recommended for hand quilting. For machine quilting, size 14 or 80 is preferred for most quilt work (size 16 or 90 for extra thick quilts).

paraffin — (see beeswax)

photocopying machine — Design elements can be manipulated, multiplied, cut and pasted, assisting the quilt designer by reducing redrawing.

pins & pincushion — T-pins or extra long quilting pins are preferred over regular straight pins because they can handle more material. Safety pins are especially helpful when using small quilt frames or hoops; have several dozen safety pins on hand.

protractor — This one is another geometry class leftover that will be useful when designing original blocks or enlarging patterns.

quilting frame or hoop — These tools hold the work flat and even as the quilting is done. Full size frames have an advantage over the small hoops as the material remains locked in one position throughout the process, therefore minimizing any creeping of the layers. Small hoops or lap frames come in a variety of sizes. Their advantages are convenience and mobility. They are especially useful for quilting in small quarters, but beware of the bunching and unevenness that can occur in the quilt after frequent repositionings.

rotary cutter & mat — Many quilters regard these tools as the most valuable gadgets since the invention of the sewing machine. Rotary cutters generally come in two sizes — small and large. Mats also come in a variety of sizes and grid patterns. Used together, a rotary cutter and mat allow you to cut many layers of fabric at once, and with greater accuracy than shears provide.

ruler — A variety of rulers is often an asset. A clear acrylic quilter's ruler is thick and durable. Most often marked with a 1-inch grid and a 45° mark, the quilter's ruler helps measure, mark and cut at the same time. A 6-inch ruler with 1/4-inch markings will come in handy when quilting along edges in a quilt block. A yard stick is helpful when measuring for borders and bindings.

sewing machine (optional) — If you have chosen to machine quilt, be sure to have your machine in good working order, several bobbins wound beforehand, and some sewing machine oil on hand to keep gears running smoothly.

scissors — Regular household scissors, for cutting templates from plastic or cardboard, will keep away the temptation to use the good dressmaker's shears.

shears — Long-bladed dressmaker's shears are necessary for cutting material cleanly.

template material — Templates can be cut from cardboard, pasteboard or plastic. Some quilters affix fine sandpaper to the back of template pieces to prevent them from slipping during the cutting process. Plastic templates wear better than cardboard counterparts.

thimble — Metal, leather or plastic, all varieties of thimbles are readily available; selection is a matter of personal preference. Rubber finger tips, sold at office supply centers, can also be used as thimbles and are helpful in gripping and pulling the needle through multiple layers of a quilt.

thread — For *hand quilting* there are two choices of thread. Cotton quilting thread is preferred but is sometimes hard to find. Cotton covered polyester core thread is usually more readily available and comes in various weights; 50 and 70 are the most popular choices.

For *machine quilting*, use regular machine sewing thread. Choose cotton thread for cotton fabric and cotton blend for synthetic fabrics whenever possible.

Note: *In either case, selecting thread of the highest quality available should be a quilter's top priority.*

tissue or tracing paper — For tracing patterns this "see-through" paper is invaluable.

tracing wheel & carbon — These two items used together are useful for tracing general quilt top stitching patterns.

Cleaning

Considering the time and effort involved in quilt making, preservation is of utmost concern. Frequent airing of a stored quilt is recommended. When "airing out" the quilt on a clothesline, be sure to evenly distribute the weight by spreading the quilt over several lines.

Every quilt will occasionally need cleaning. If you assembled the quilt yourself you should know the stability and color-fastness of the fabric. If you acquired the quilt another way and do not know the particulars about the fabrics used, do some testing first.

Take the age of the quilt into consideration. The older the quilt, the greater care necessary in cleaning it. Very old fragile quilts are best entrusted to professionals. Check with historical museum curators for such advice. Even a quilt from the early 20th century, such as your great-grandma's quilt, should be examined thoroughly before washing. If you can tell that the quilt contains wool or silk, it should be dry cleaned.

If the quilt is determined to be structurally sound, having strong stitches and sturdy cotton or cotton/poly blend fabric and filling, take a few moments to ensure color fastness. Put a few drops of water on an inconspicuous area of the quilt and blot it with a white cloth. If no "bleeding" occurs, try again with a mixture of mild detergent and water. Repeat this test in various areas of the quilt, on different patches of material. Color fastness varies from fabric to fabric so make no assumptions.

Be especially careful with dark and bright swatches. If the white cloth shows no sign of the other colors, you can probably assume it is safe to hand wash the quilt. If, however, the dye is determined unstable, dry cleaning will be your only option.

For even the most sturdy quilts, hand washing with a mild detergent is preferred. With piecing and stitching there is risk of damage when using a washing machine. The strong agitation tends to pull and tear out stitches while the powerful laundry detergents can wear down fabrics. Reckless washing can lead to tears, fading colors and harmful detergent residues.

Add a mild detergent (specifically for delicate fabrics) to lukewarm water in a large sink or bathtub. Immerse the quilt and gently agitate with your hands. Usually, these "hand wash" detergents advise a short soaking time of 15 to 30 minutes, which is fine. Finally, drain the water and refill the tub, still gently agitating to work out suds and rinse. Continue this process two or three times, or until the water runs clear.

Once the soap is completely removed, drain the tub, pressing out as much water as possible. Resist the temptation to wring the quilt. Folding and rolling the quilt is less stressful to the stitching. Also, the wet quilt will be surprisingly heavy, so you may want help removing it from the tub. Extra hands when lifting will create a more even weight distribution, thereby avoiding tears.

If you use a clothesline for drying, do not hang the wet quilt by one end. Doing so will put too much strain on the stitching; be sure to spread the quilt across several lines. A more advisable drying method is to lay a sheet on the grass and spread the quilt on top, avoiding direct sunlight that may strip color.

Storage

Do not store quilts in plastic bags; textiles need to "breathe." Instead, wrap them loosely in clean cotton sheets. To prevent discoloration, prolonged exposure to sunlight and contact with wood surfaces should be avoided. Also, refold stored quilts every couple of months to prevent permanent creasing. Before handling stored quilts be sure that your hands are freshly washed to remove natural oils that can stain with the passing of time.

To hang a quilt for display, create a long narrow sleeve of unsized cotton, the length of which equals the width of the quilt along its top edge. This sleeve should be sewn and attached with small stitches, for extra strength. Be sure that the stitches penetrate deeply into the quilt layers as you attach the sleeve.

Finally, a wooden or metal rod can be inserted through this sleeve, to hang the quilt on a wall. Although there are many other methods to hang a quilt, this one is the most widely accepted. Some old quilts may be too fragile to hang with this method, however, and will require the attachment of an additional lining. Simply baste a stronger fabric, prewashed to remove sizing, to the back of the quilt and hang it with the lining bearing the weight. Keep in mind that there are many vintage quilts that are just too heavy or fragile to hang at all.

Often, individual collectors will display their treasures on a guestroom bed, layering one quilt on top of another. They are then rotated periodically, allowing air movement while creating a constantly changing display of color and style.

Dove In The Window

This quilt design is made up primarily of diamond shapes that are stitched to form an eight-pointed star, similar to a design called "Star of Lemoyne" or "Lemon Star." Unlike the plain eight-pointed star, however, "Dove In The Window," gives the added dimension of birds resting beak-to-beak. The design is said to have gotten its name from the pigeons who used to roost in the windows built near the rafters of old barns. The quilt design might also be called "Birds of a Feather," however, since the birds seem to be flocking together in the quilt squares.

Materials: Standard quilting items from supplies checklist and fabric scraps in colors indicated on pattern (or select your own preferred colors).

Finished Measurements: One finished quilt block measures 17-1/2 x 17-1/2 inches (minus seam allowance); finished quilt measures five blocks wide and six blocks long, or 87-1/2 x 105

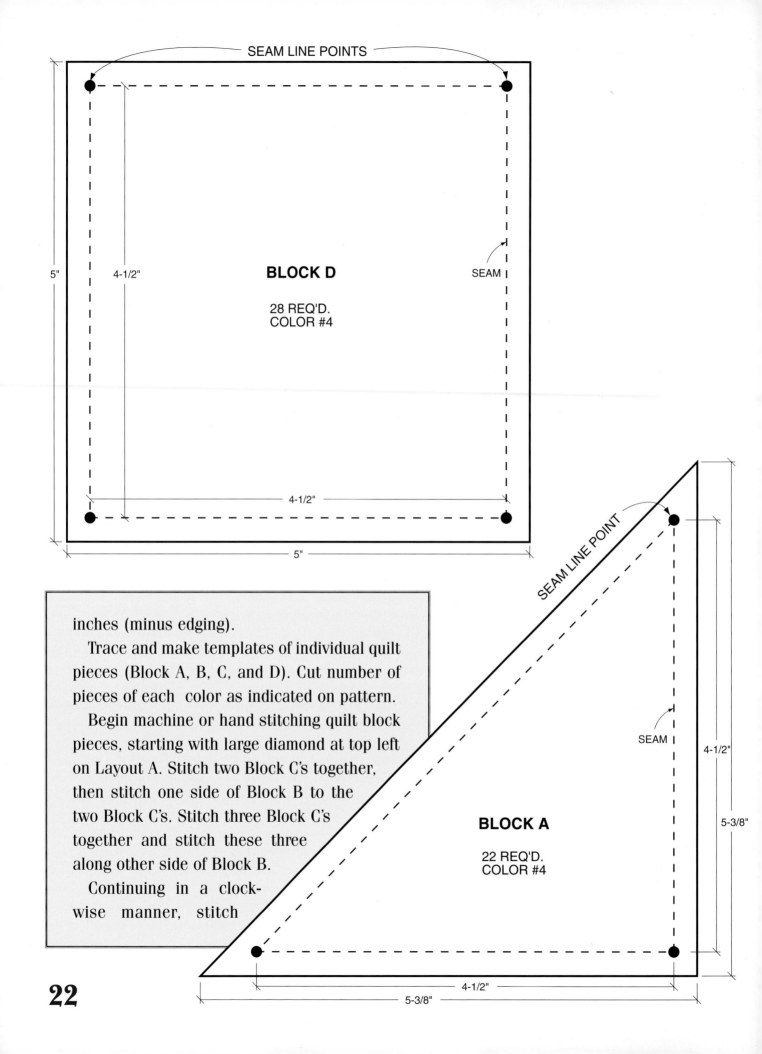

SEAM LINE POINTS

BLOCK D

28 REQ'D.
COLOR #4

5"

4-1/2"

SEAM

4-1/2"

5"

inches (minus edging).

Trace and make templates of individual quilt pieces (Block A, B, C, and D). Cut number of pieces of each color as indicated on pattern.

Begin machine or hand stitching quilt block pieces, starting with large diamond at top left on Layout A. Stitch two Block C's together, then stitch one side of Block B to the two Block C's. Stitch three Block C's together and stitch these three along other side of Block B.

Continuing in a clockwise manner, stitch

SEAM LINE POINT

BLOCK A

22 REQ'D.
COLOR #4

SEAM

4-1/2"

5-3/8"

4-1/2"

5-3/8"

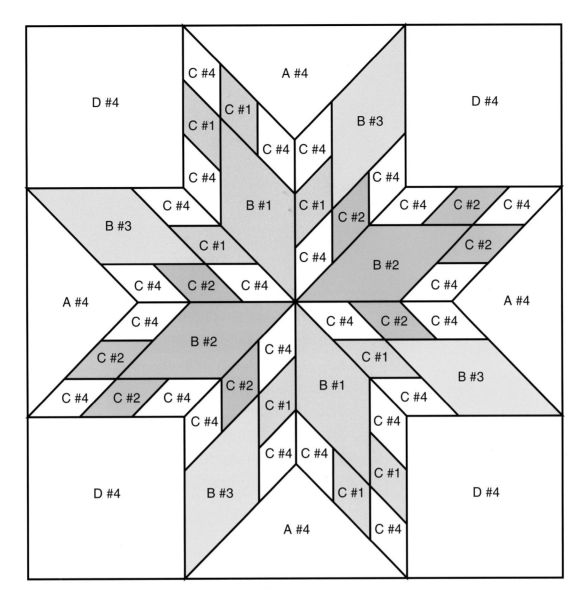

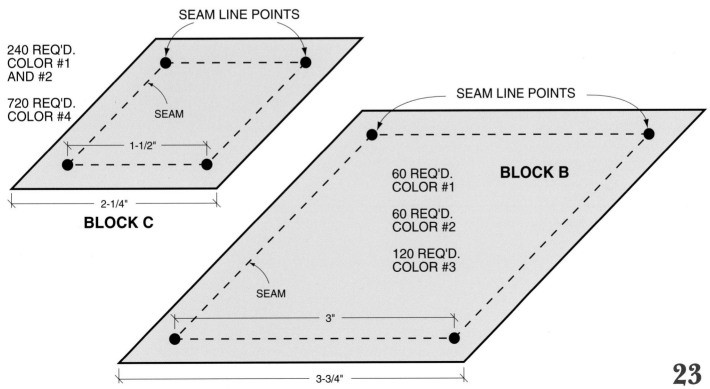

SEAM LINE POINTS

240 REQ'D.
COLOR #1
AND #2

720 REQ'D.
COLOR #4

SEAM

1-1/2"

2-1/4"

BLOCK C

SEAM LINE POINTS

BLOCK B

60 REQ'D.
COLOR #1

60 REQ'D.
COLOR #2

120 REQ'D.
COLOR #3

SEAM

3"

3-3/4"

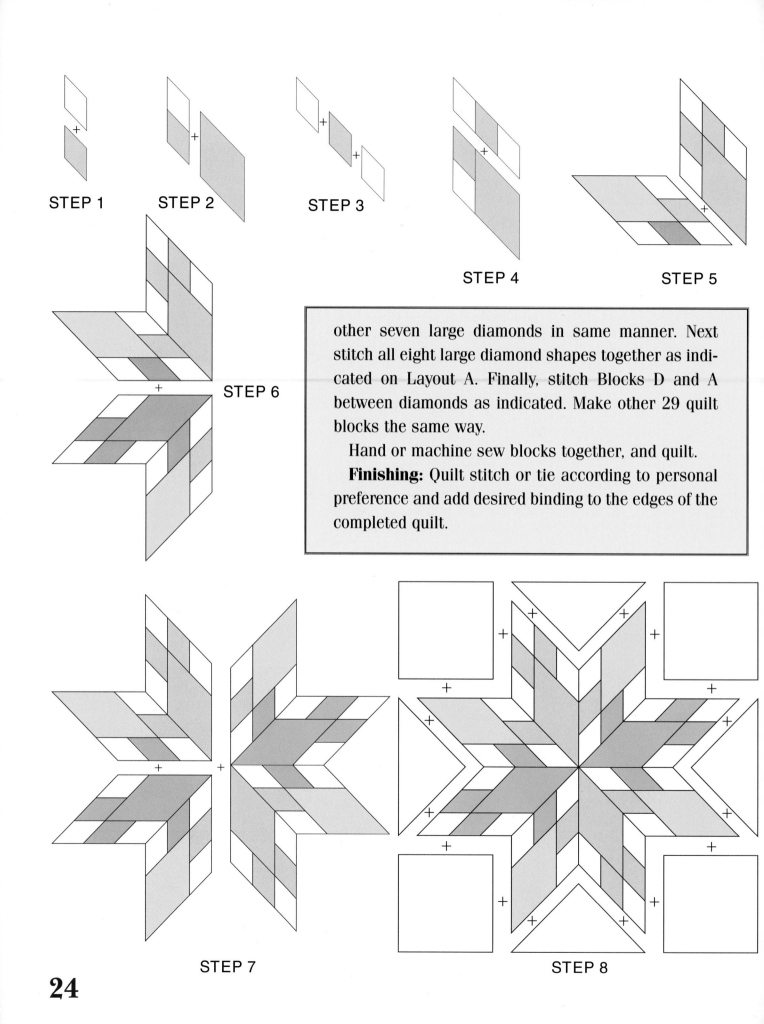

STEP 1

STEP 2

STEP 3

STEP 4

STEP 5

STEP 6

other seven large diamonds in same manner. Next stitch all eight large diamond shapes together as indicated on Layout A. Finally, stitch Blocks D and A between diamonds as indicated. Make other 29 quilt blocks the same way.

Hand or machine sew blocks together, and quilt.

Finishing: Quilt stitch or tie according to personal preference and add desired binding to the edges of the completed quilt.

STEP 7

STEP 8

25

Ohio Star

This Nine Patch design is made up of squares and triangles stitched to form an eight-pointed star. The completed quilt contains two variations of the block, which are set in a checkerboard fashion. The set blocks are then framed with multiple Amish-style borders, enhancing the simple beauty of this Ohio Star quilt.

FULL QUILT BLOCK A

K #1	J #1	K #1
	I #2 I #2	
I #2		I #2
J #1	M #2	J #1
I #2		I #2
K #1	I #2 J #1 I #2	K #1

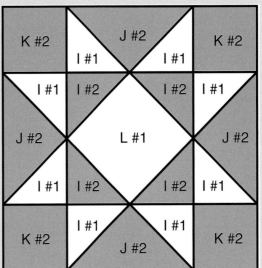

FULL QUILT BLOCK B

Finished Measurements: One finished quilt block measures 10 x 10 inches (minus seam allowance); the finished quilt measures five blocks wide and seven blocks long, or 72 x 92 inches, with borders added (minus edging).

Cut the number of pieces of each color as indicated on the pattern. Start machine or hand stitching the quilt block pieces, following the step-by-step diagrams. Make 17 quilt blocks according to layout A and 18 quilt blocks according to layout B.

Stitch the blocks together in rows. Be sure to begin three rows with an A block, and four rows with a B block. Pin corners first, followed by seams, then stitch with short running

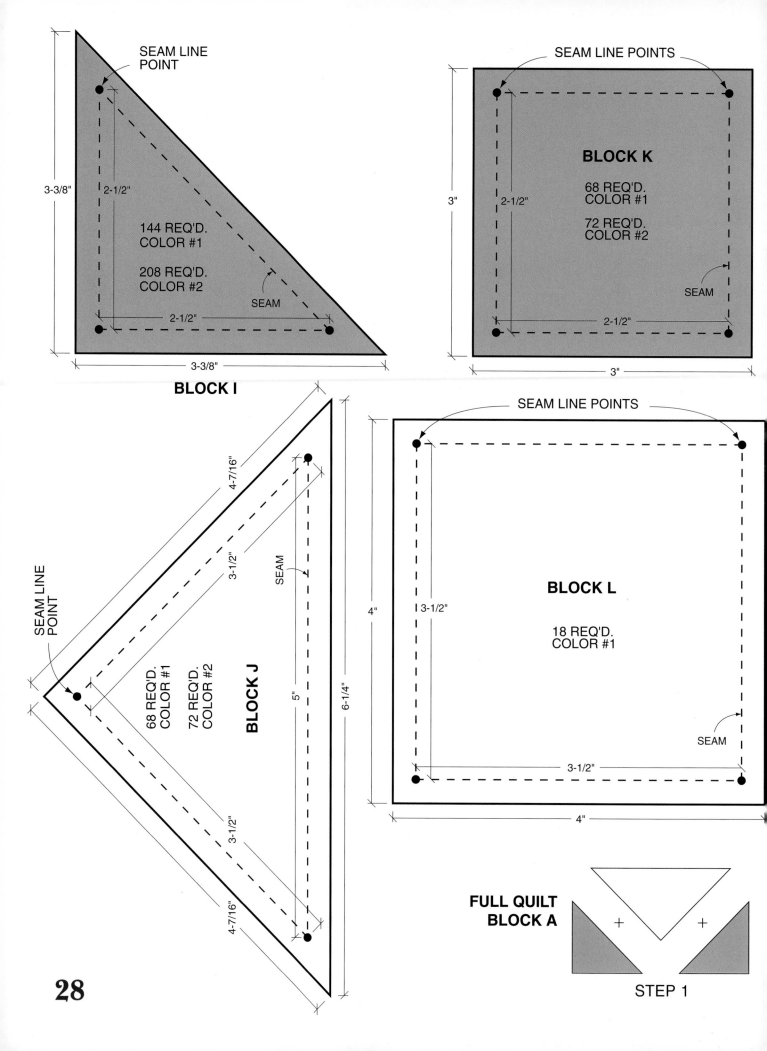

SEAM LINE
POINT

3-3/8"

2-1/2"

144 REQ'D.
COLOR #1

208 REQ'D.
COLOR #2

SEAM

2-1/2"

3-3/8"

BLOCK I

SEAM LINE POINTS

BLOCK K

68 REQ'D.
COLOR #1

72 REQ'D.
COLOR #2

3"

2-1/2"

SEAM

2-1/2"

3"

SEAM LINE
POINT

4-7/16"

3-1/2"

SEAM

5"

6-1/4"

68 REQ'D.
COLOR #1

72 REQ'D.
COLOR #2

BLOCK J

3-1/2"

4-7/16"

SEAM LINE POINTS

BLOCK L

18 REQ'D.
COLOR #1

4"

3-1/2"

SEAM

3-1/2"

4"

**FULL QUILT
BLOCK A**

STEP 1

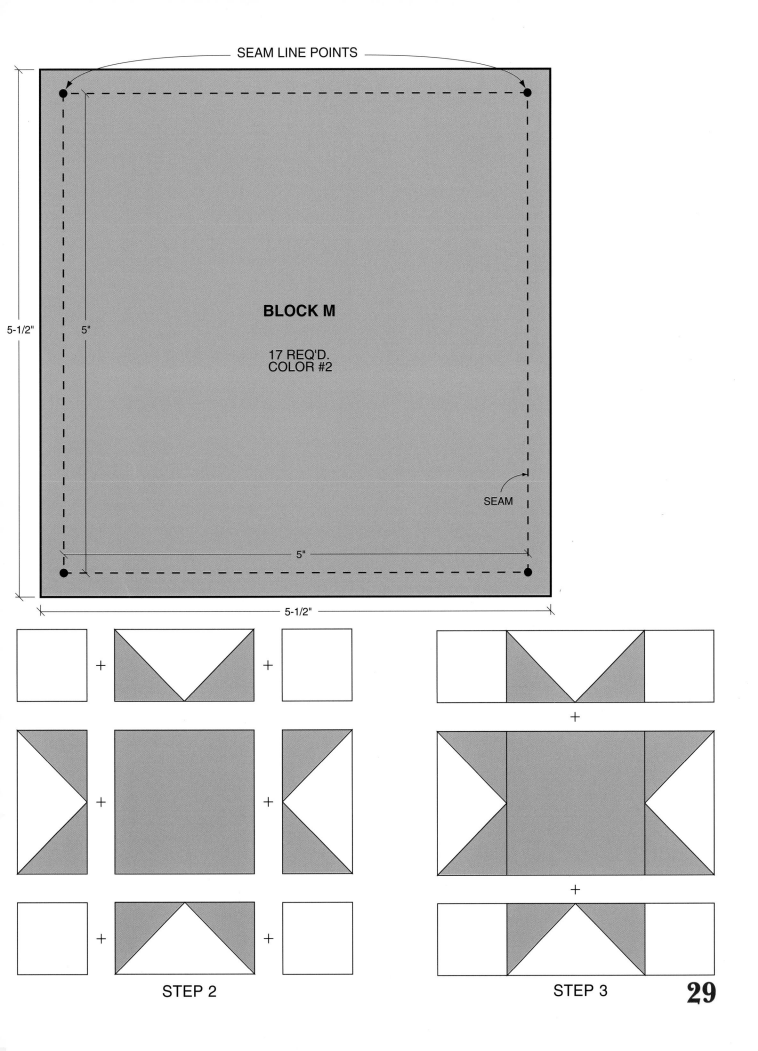

SEAM LINE POINTS

BLOCK M

17 REQ'D.
COLOR #2

5-1/2"

5"

5"

SEAM

5-1/2"

STEP 2

STEP 3

29

FULL QUILT
BLOCK B

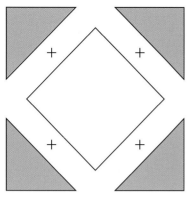

STEP 1

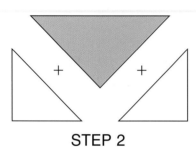

STEP 2

stitches. Join finished rows, alternating according to the quilt diagram, and stitching two together at a time. Be sure to match vertical seams before sewing.

Apply borders in alphabetic sequence, according to the quilt diagram.

Finishing: Quilt or tie according to personal preference and add desired binding to edges of completed quilt.

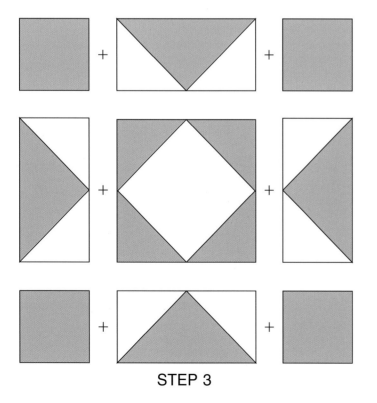

STEP 3

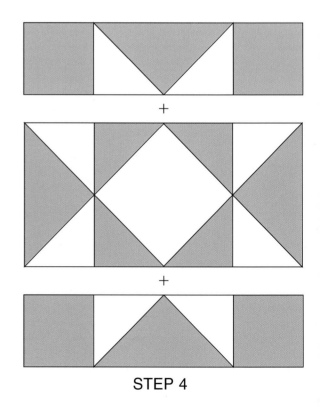

STEP 4

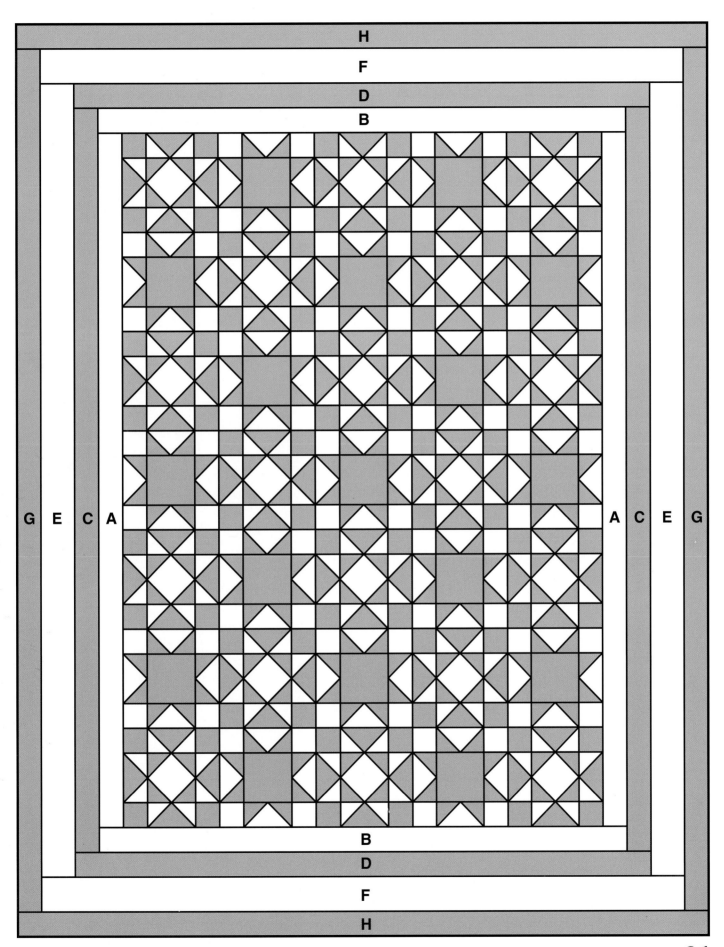

Wheel of Fortune

*T*his quilt design is made up of tiny square blocks that are divided into two equal triangles with petal shapes stitched into their corners. As these small blocks are joined, little "wheels" appear. This almost magical occurrence is undoubtedly source of its name — Wheel of Fortune. Even more magically, wheel shapes also emerge as additional rows of blocks are set.

Finished Measurements: One finished quilt block measures 4-1/4 x 4-1/4 inches (minus seam allowance); the finished quilt measures 16 blocks wide and 18 blocks long, or 68 x 76-1/2 inches (minus edging).

Cut the number of pieces of each color as indicated on the pattern. Start machine or hand stitching quilt block pieces, following the step-by-step diagrams. Clip inside curves of the pieces to make it easier to sew curved pieces together, being careful that you don't cut into the seam line. Make all 288 quilt blocks in the same manner.

Stitch the blocks together in fours as indicated. Be sure to match the corner seam points

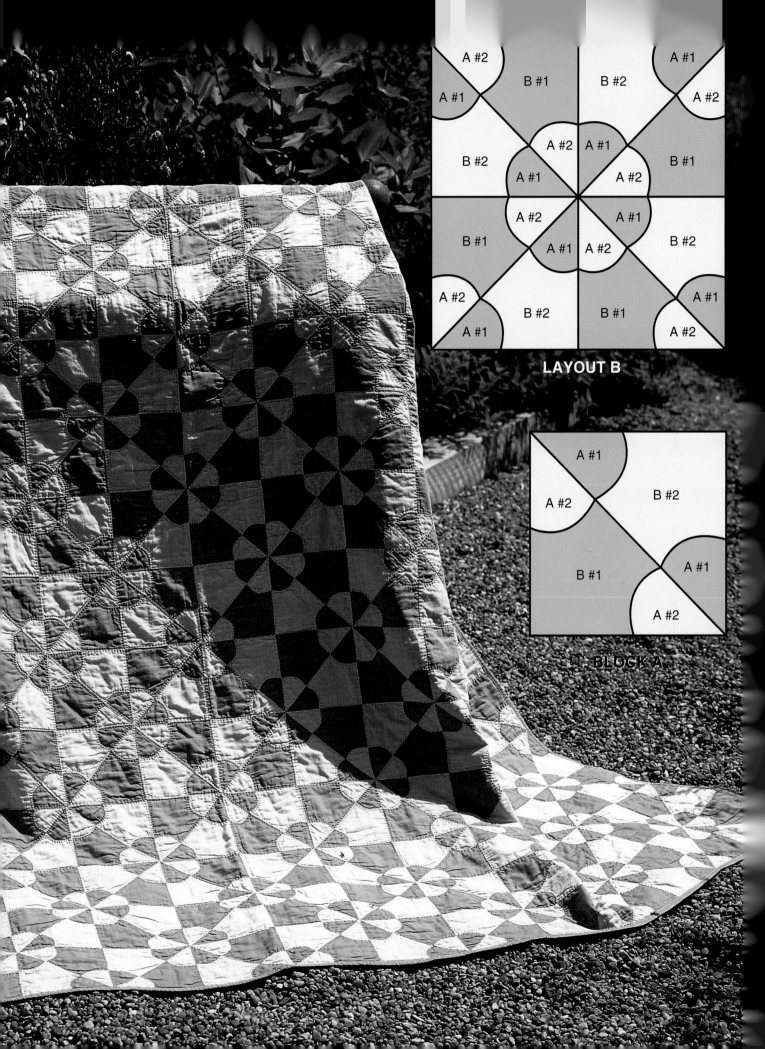

LAYOUT B

BLOCK A

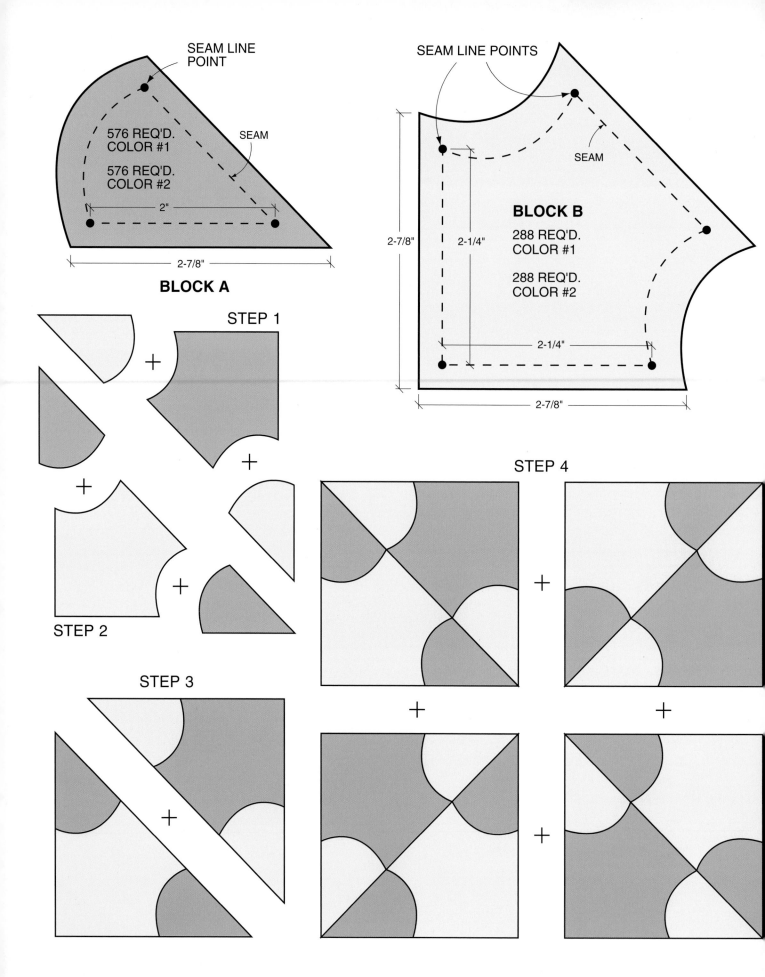

SEAM LINE
POINT

576 REQ'D.
COLOR #1

576 REQ'D.
COLOR #2

SEAM

2"

2-7/8"

BLOCK A

SEAM LINE POINTS

SEAM

BLOCK B
288 REQ'D.
COLOR #1

288 REQ'D.
COLOR #2

2-7/8"

2-1/4"

2-1/4"

2-7/8"

STEP 1

+

+

+

STEP 2

+

STEP 3

+

STEP 4

+

+

+

+

34

when joining, so a smooth "wheel" is formed, as shown. Stitch the wheel blocks together, forming rows of eight wheel blocks. Pin corners first, followed by seams, then stitch with short running stitches. Join finished rows two at a time, matching vertical seams before sewing.

Finishing: Quilt or tie according to personal preference and add desired binding to edges of completed quilt.

Fan Patchwork

Popular as a *friendship quilt*, this pattern requires quite a large and varied stash of fabric scraps to complete. In times of scarcity, friends would share their bits and pieces of leftover fabric. Quilts, such as the Fan Patchwork design, were the brilliant result. When cut and pieced, these colorful scraps form the panels of the fan. White fabric is then cut and stitched to fill the remaining area of the block.

Finished Measurements: One finished quilt block measures 8 x 8 inches (minus seam allowance); the finished quilt measures 10 blocks wide and 12 blocks long, or 80 x 96 inches (minus edging).

Cut the number of pieces of each color as indicated on the pattern. Start machine or hand stitching the quilt block pieces, following the step-by-step diagrams. Make all 120 quilt blocks in the same manner.

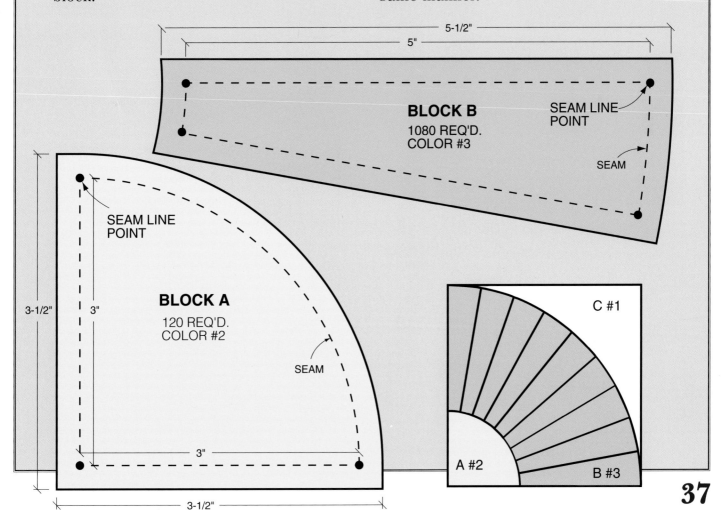

BLOCK B
1080 REQ'D.
COLOR #3

SEAM LINE POINT

SEAM

5-1/2"

5"

SEAM LINE POINT

BLOCK A
120 REQ'D.
COLOR #2

SEAM

3-1/2"

3"

3"

3-1/2"

C #1

A #2

B #3

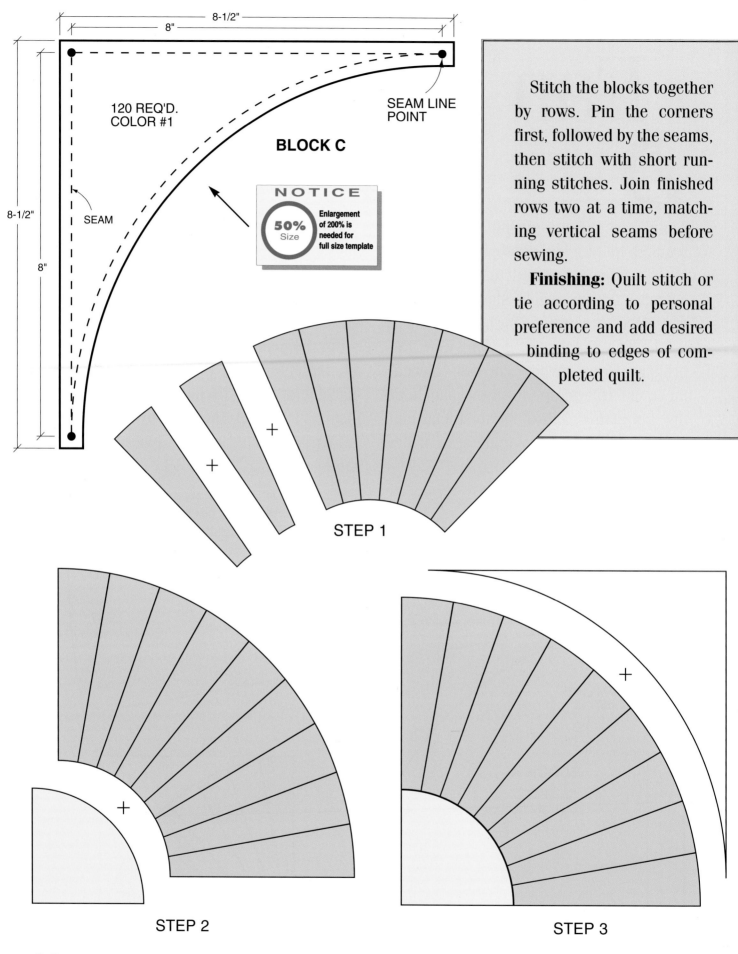

8-1/2"

8"

120 REQ'D.
COLOR #1

8-1/2"

8"

SEAM

BLOCK C

SEAM LINE
POINT

NOTICE

50% Size

Enlargement of 200% is needed for full size template

Stitch the blocks together by rows. Pin the corners first, followed by the seams, then stitch with short running stitches. Join finished rows two at a time, matching vertical seams before sewing.

Finishing: Quilt stitch or tie according to personal preference and add desired binding to edges of completed quilt.

STEP 1

STEP 2

STEP 3

38

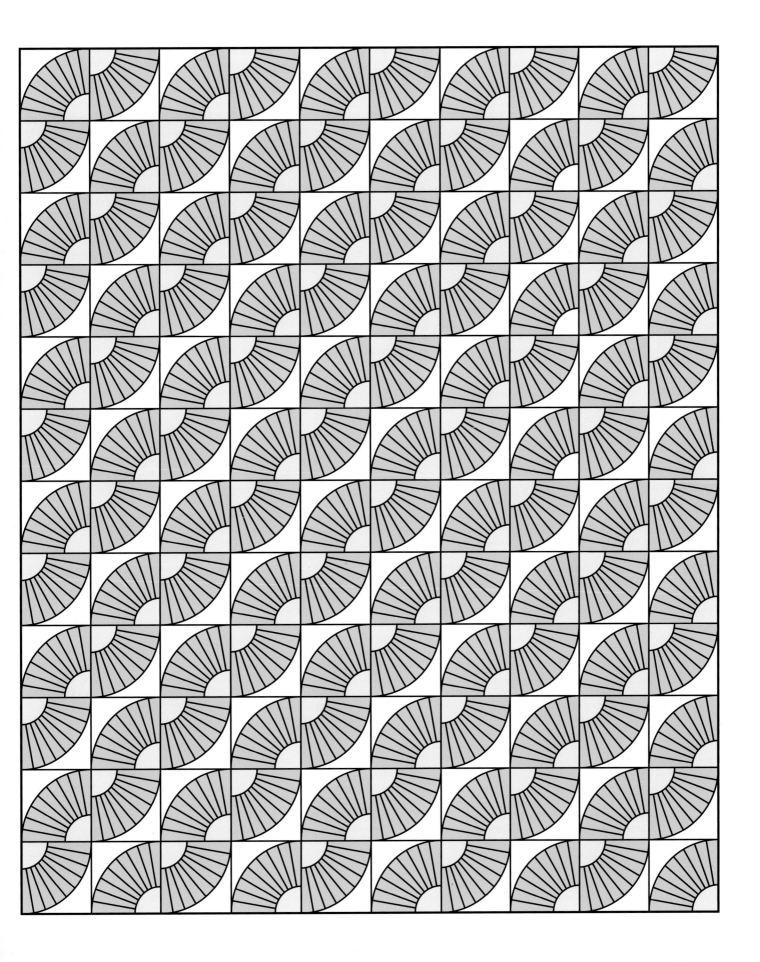

Dutchman's Puzzle

In this simple Four-Patch quilt block, each small square is divided into two triangles of contrasting color. With careful placement, these squares combine to form a pinwheel design. The quilt block's name Dutchman's Puzzle likely points to the heritage of its designer. However, the design itself, which somewhat resembles the blades of a windmill, is said to be derived from an ancient symbol of good luck.

Finished Measurements: One finished quilt block measures 10 x 10 inches (minus seam allowance); the finished quilt measures seven blocks wide and eight blocks long, or 76 x 80 inches after the addition of side borders (minus edging).

Cut the number of pieces of each color as indicated on the pattern. Start machine or hand stitching the quilt block pieces, following the step-by-step diagrams. Make all 28 quilt blocks in the same manner.

Stitch the blocks together in rows, alternating one pieced block with one plain block. Start four rows with pieced block and four rows with a plain block.

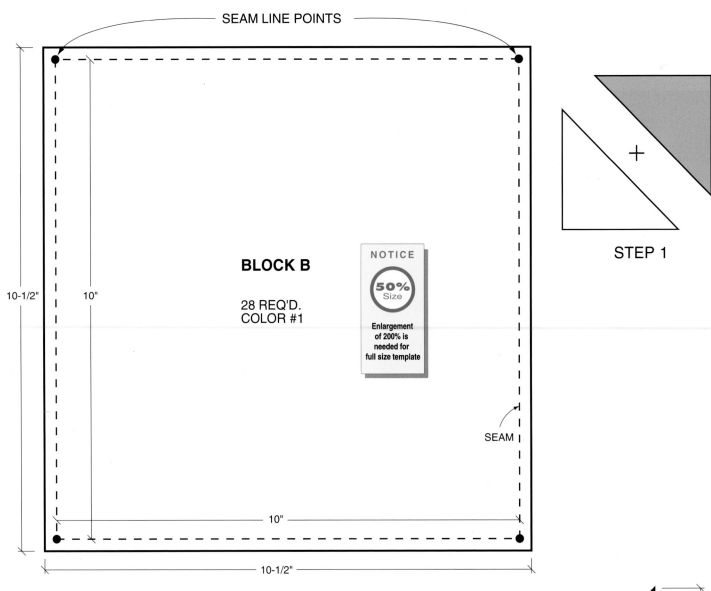

SEAM LINE POINTS

STEP 1

BLOCK B

28 REQ'D.
COLOR #1

NOTICE

50% Size

Enlargement
of 200% is
needed for
full size template

SEAM

10-1/2"

10"

10"

10-1/2"

Pin corners first, followed by the seams, then stitch with short running stitches. Join the finished rows two at a time, alternating as necessary for correct layout and matching vertical seams before sewing. Then, add borders to edges of quilt, according to the quilt diagram.

Finishing: Quilt stitch or tie according to personal preference and add desired binding to the edges of the completed quilt.

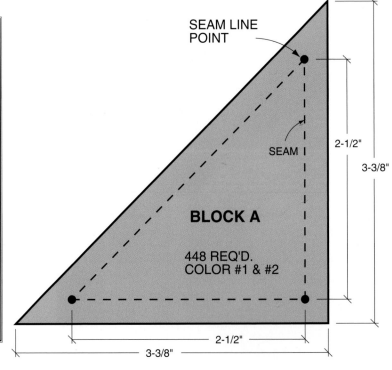

SEAM LINE
POINT

SEAM

2-1/2"

3-3/8"

BLOCK A

448 REQ'D.
COLOR #1 & #2

2-1/2"

3-3/8"

42

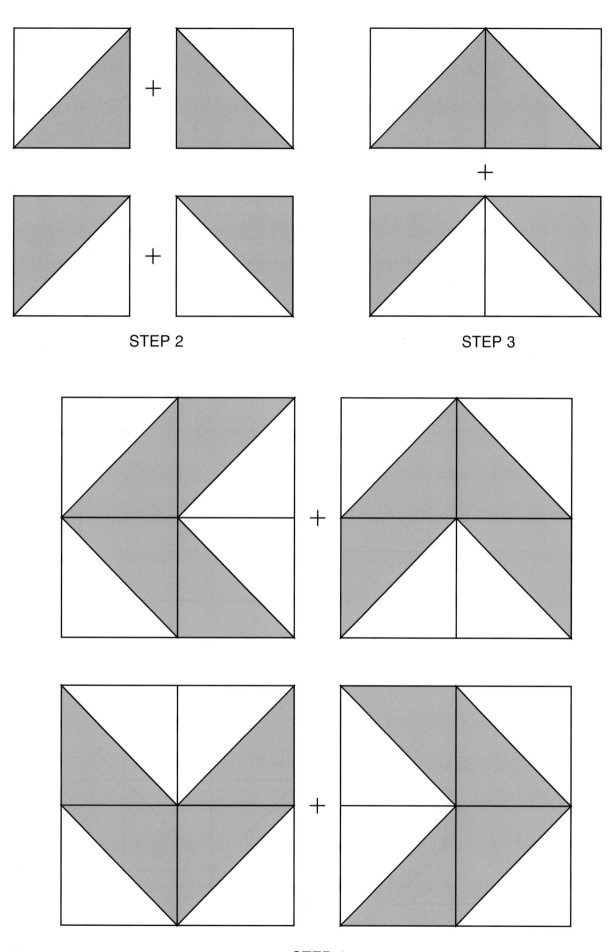

STEP 2

STEP 3

STEP 4

43

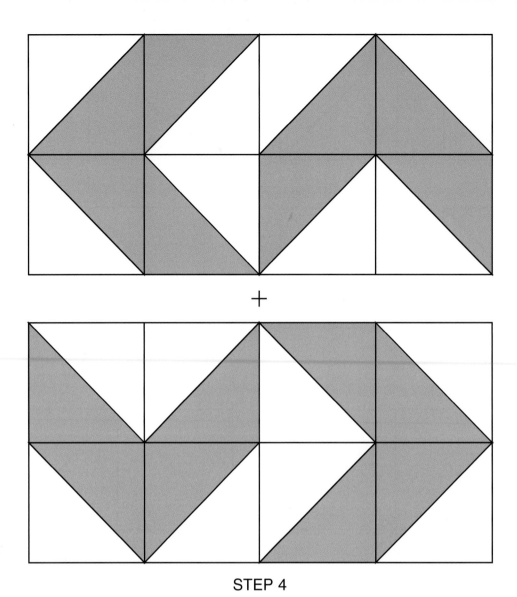

STEP 4

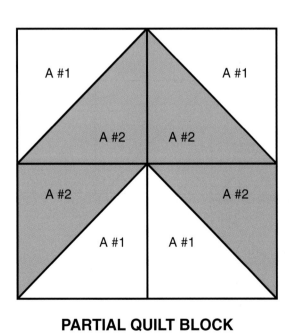

PARTIAL QUILT BLOCK

A #1	A #2	A #1	A #1
A #2	A #1	A #2	A #2
A #2	A #1	A #2	A #2
A #1	A #2	A #1	A #1
A #1	A #1	A #2	A #1
A #2	A #2	A #1	A #2
A #2	A #2	A #1	A #2
A #1	A #1	A #2	A #1

FULL QUILT BLOCK

45

Double Wedding Ring

It is said that this originally German pattern gets its name both from the rings that are formed as the quilt is set and also from the complexity of its piecing. The variety of fabrics making up the rings may symbolize how marriage blends families, as it joins two individuals. The rings intersect and unite as families do when couples marry.

Though sometimes used in the *friendship quilt* fashion, this quilt top was traditionally pieced by a young girl for her hope chest. Then, near her wedding date the quilt stitching was applied by her friends as a wedding gift.

Finished Measurements: One finished quilt block, or a *whole ring*, measures 25-3/4 x 25-3/4 inches (minus seam allowance); the finished quilt measures four *overlapping* blocks (rings) wide and four *overlapping* blocks (rings) long, or 77-1/2 x 77-1/2 inches (minus edging).

Cut the number of pieces of each fabric as indicated on the pattern. Start machine stitching the quilt block pieces, following the step-by-step diagrams. Assemble

the quilt blocks according to steps 5, 6, and 7. You will notice that there are blocks (rings) that appear to be at three levels of completion, because they will share the *missing* lemon-shaped sections with neighboring blocks.

Stitch the blocks together, carefully applying partial ones as directed. Pin seams and clip inside curves, as necessary, to ease piecing. Stitch with short running stitches. Join the finished rows two at a time.

Note: If necessary to ease fitting, adjust block B pieces (where they meet other B pieces).

Finishing: Quilt stitch according to personal preference. Then, add desired binding to edges of completed quilt.

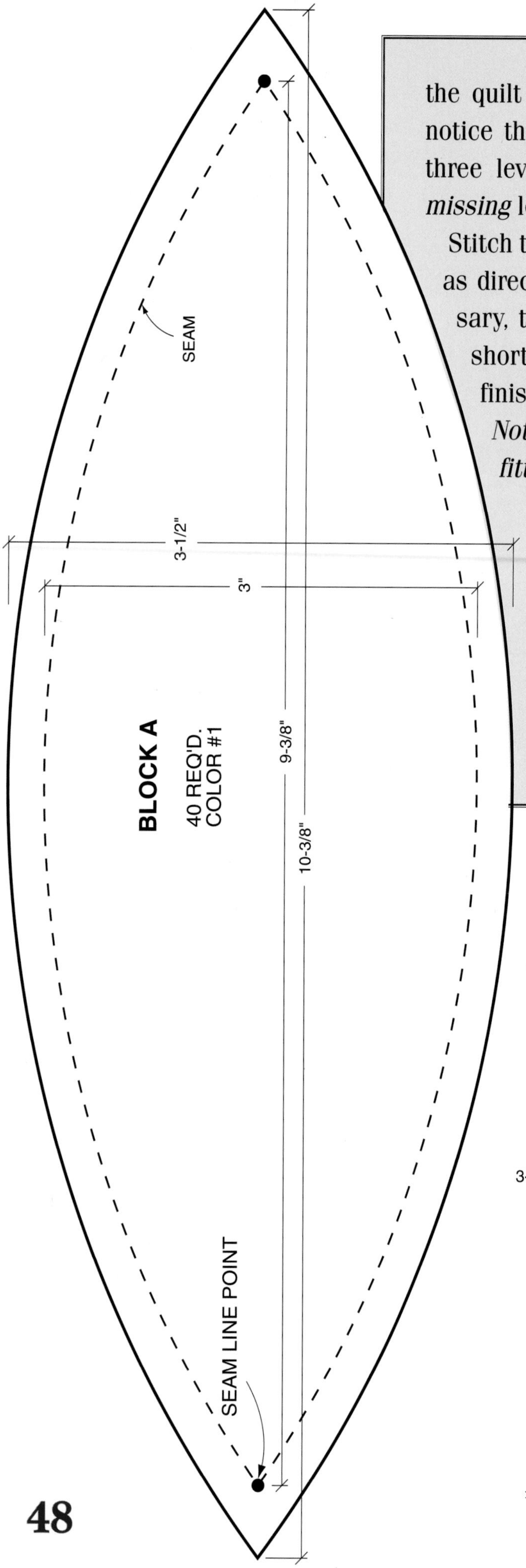

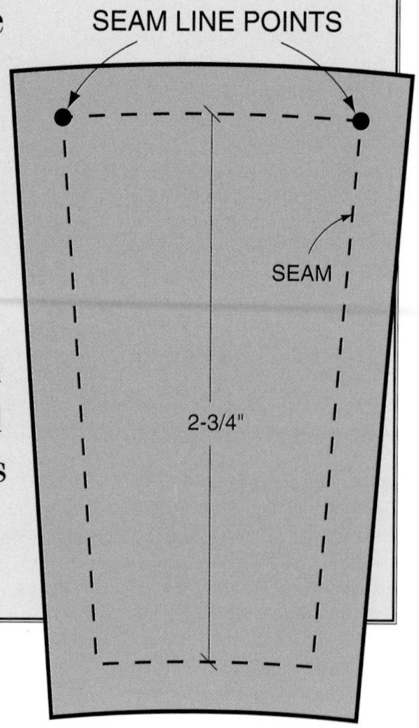

SEAM

3-1/2"

3"

9-3/8"

10-3/8"

BLOCK A

40 REQ'D.
COLOR #1

SEAM LINE POINT

SEAM LINE POINTS

SEAM

2-3/4"

BLOCK C

720 REQ'D.
COLOR #2

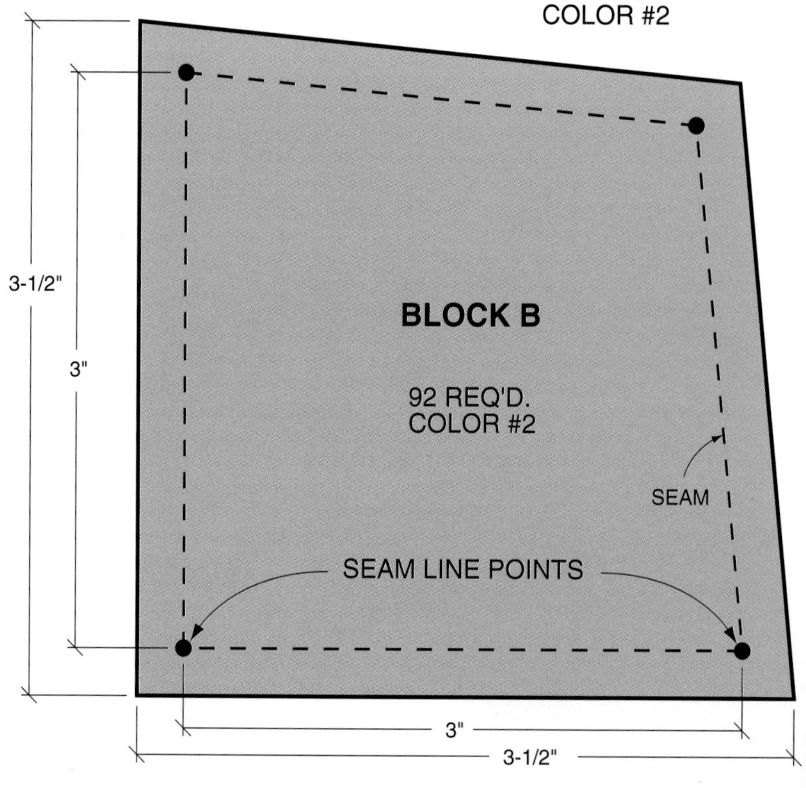

3-1/2"

3"

BLOCK B

92 REQ'D.
COLOR #2

SEAM

SEAM LINE POINTS

3"

3-1/2"

48

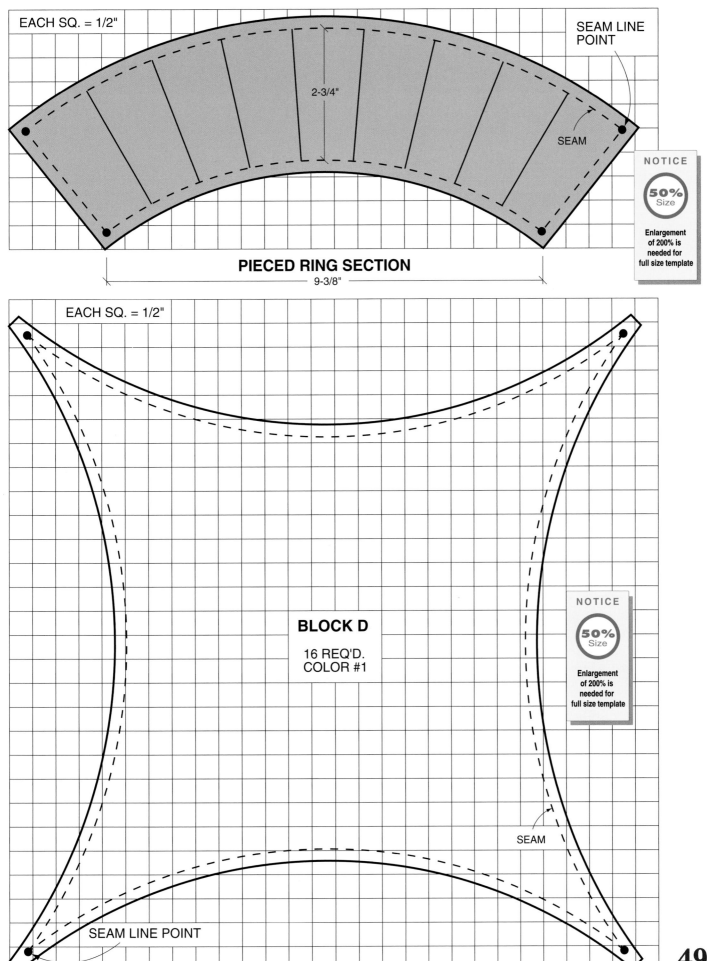

EACH SQ. = 1/2"

SEAM LINE POINT

2-3/4"

SEAM

NOTICE
50% Size
Enlargement of 200% is needed for full size template

PIECED RING SECTION

9-3/8"

EACH SQ. = 1/2"

NOTICE
50% Size
Enlargement of 200% is needed for full size template

BLOCK D

16 REQ'D.
COLOR #1

SEAM

SEAM LINE POINT

49

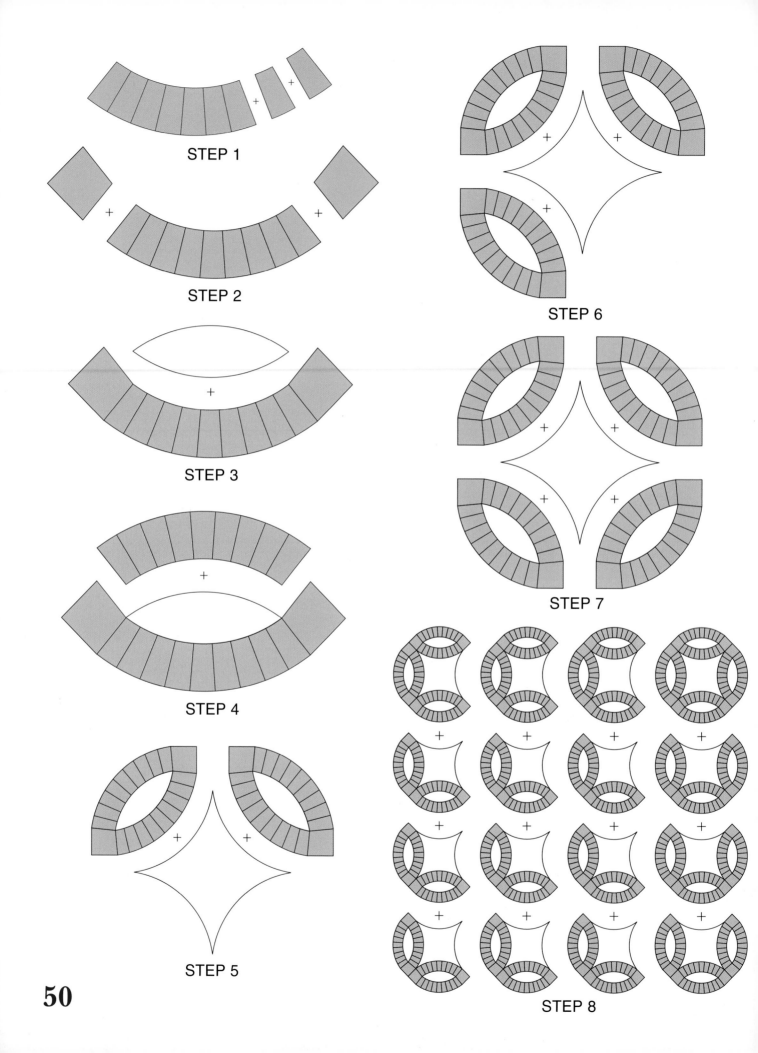

STEP 1

STEP 2

STEP 3

STEP 4

STEP 5

STEP 6

STEP 7

STEP 8

50

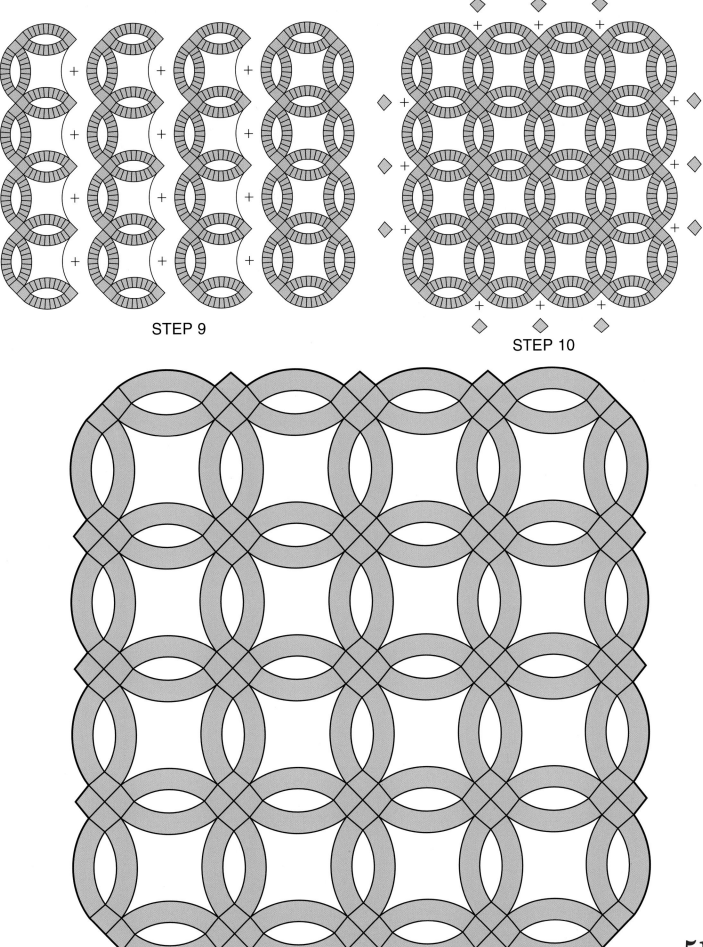

STEP 9

STEP 10

51

Purple Cross

*T*his quilt block pattern combines the straight lines and angular pieces of an eight pointed star block with the round edges of a circular style pattern. The result is a colorful block that is a bit of a challenge to piece.

Ordinarily, a quilter could feel satisfaction, having successfully pieced an eight pointed star. The maker of the "Purple Cross" can not yet be content, though, and now faces the task of carefully fitting the circle curve that surrounds the star.

Finished Measurements: One finished quilt block measures 11 x 11 inches (minus seam allowance); the finished quilt measures seven blocks wide and nine blocks long, or 77 x 99 inches (minus edging).

Cut number of pieces of each color as indicated on pattern. Start machine or hand stitching quilt block pieces, following step-by-step diagrams. Be sure to use the seam line points when matching

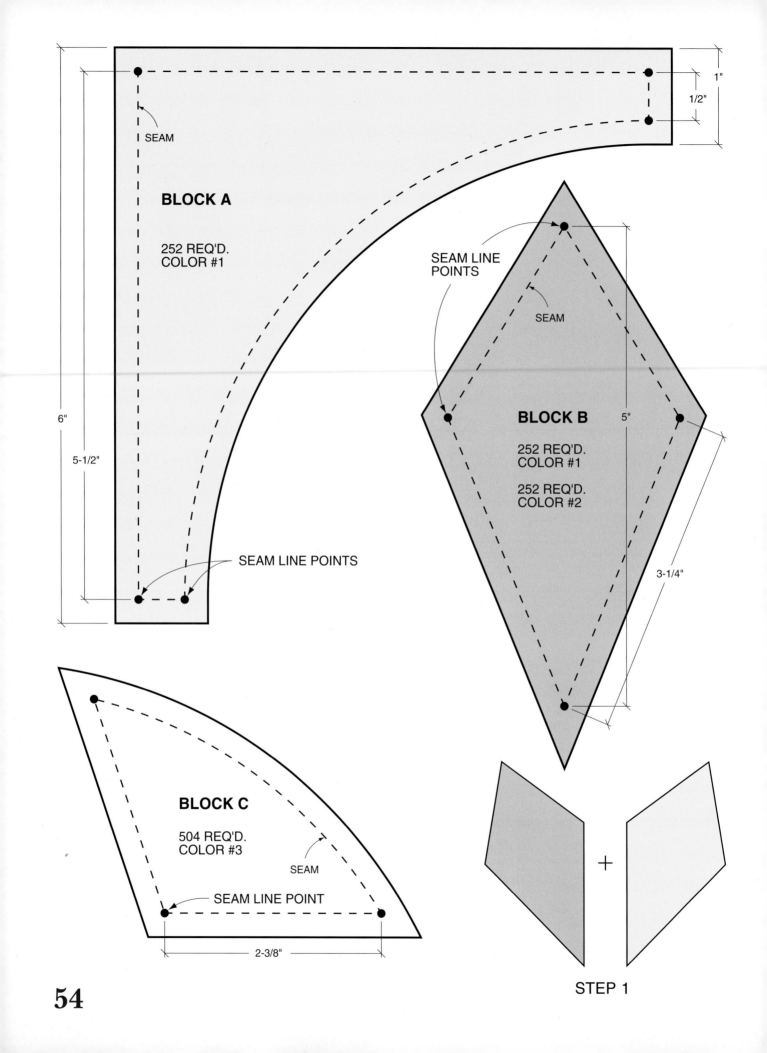

SEAM

BLOCK A

252 REQ'D.
COLOR #1

SEAM LINE POINTS

1"

1/2"

SEAM LINE
POINTS

SEAM

BLOCK B

252 REQ'D.
COLOR #1

252 REQ'D.
COLOR #2

5"

3-1/4"

6"

5-1/2"

BLOCK C

504 REQ'D.
COLOR #3

SEAM

SEAM LINE POINT

2-3/8"

+

STEP 1

54

pieces, and clip inside curves when piecing curved pieces. Make all 63 quilt blocks in the same manner.

Stitch blocks together by rows. Pin corners first, followed by seams, then stitch with short running stitches. Join finished rows two at a time, matching vertical seams before sewing.

Finishing: Quilt stitch or tie, then add desired binding to edges of the completed quilt.

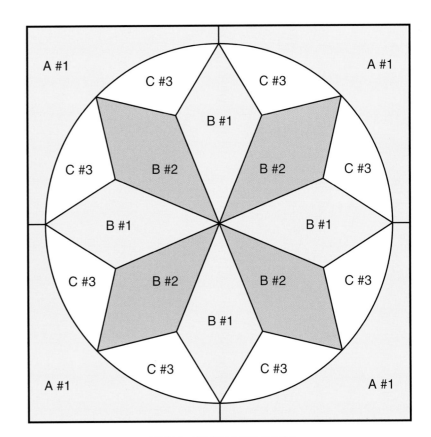

FULL QUILT BLOCK

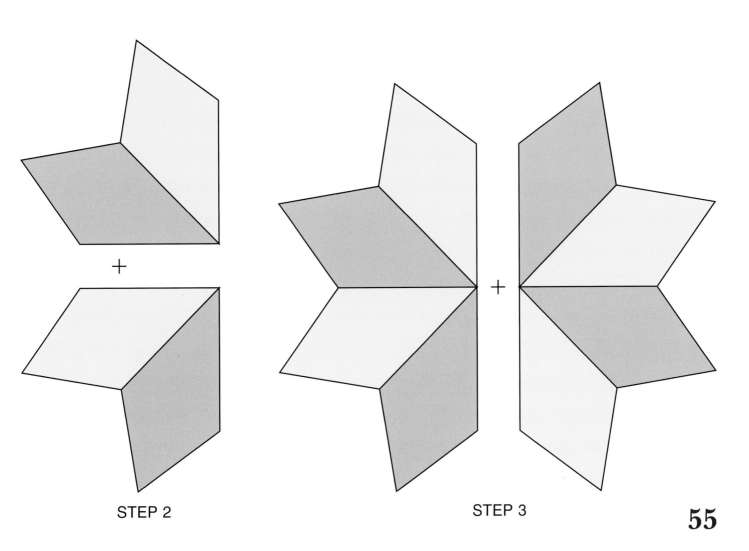

STEP 2

STEP 3

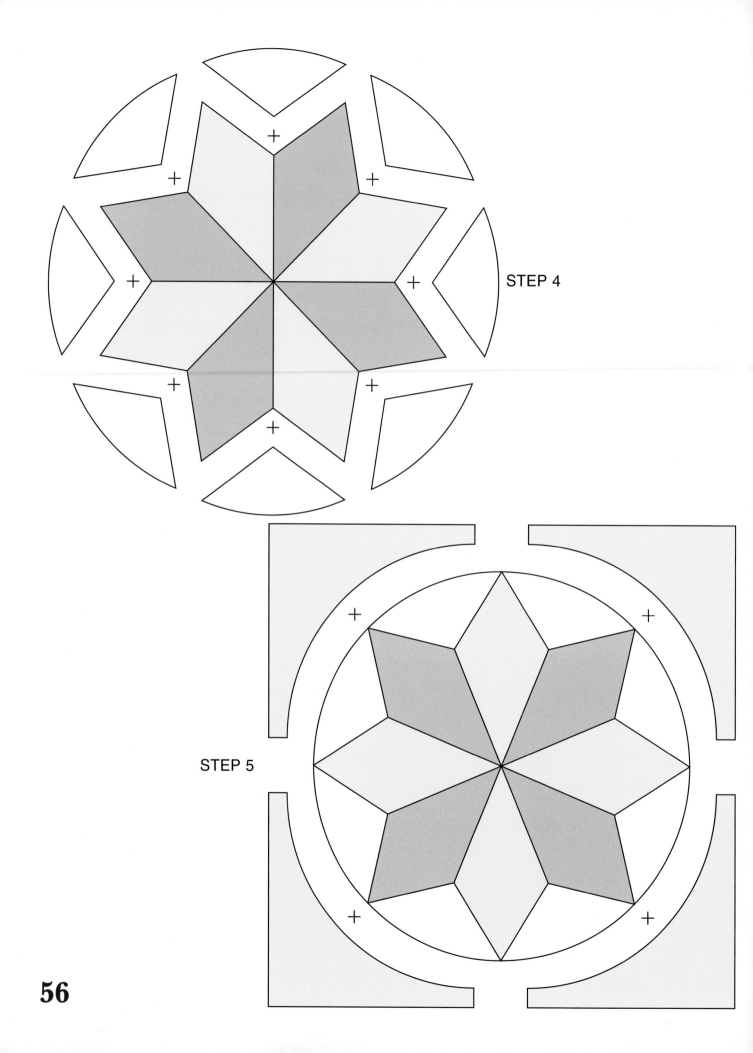

STEP 4

STEP 5

56

57

Four Patch

The Four Patch pattern is not only one of the simplest of the pieced quilt blocks, but it is the forerunner of many other quilt patterns. Most blocks are based on the One Patch, the Four Patch, or the Nine Patch design. From these simple beginnings, each segment can be divided into smaller segments, producing unlimited variations. This pattern, however, shows the Four Patch in its purest form and is an excellent choice for the beginning quilter.

Finished Measurements: One finished quilt block measures 10 x 10 inches (minus seam allowance); the finished quilt measures six blocks wide and eight blocks long, or 66 x 79 inches, with the border added and edges hemmed.

Cut the number of pieces of each color as indicated on the pattern. Start machine or hand stitching the quilt block pieces, following step-by-step diagrams. Make 24 quilt blocks in the same manner.

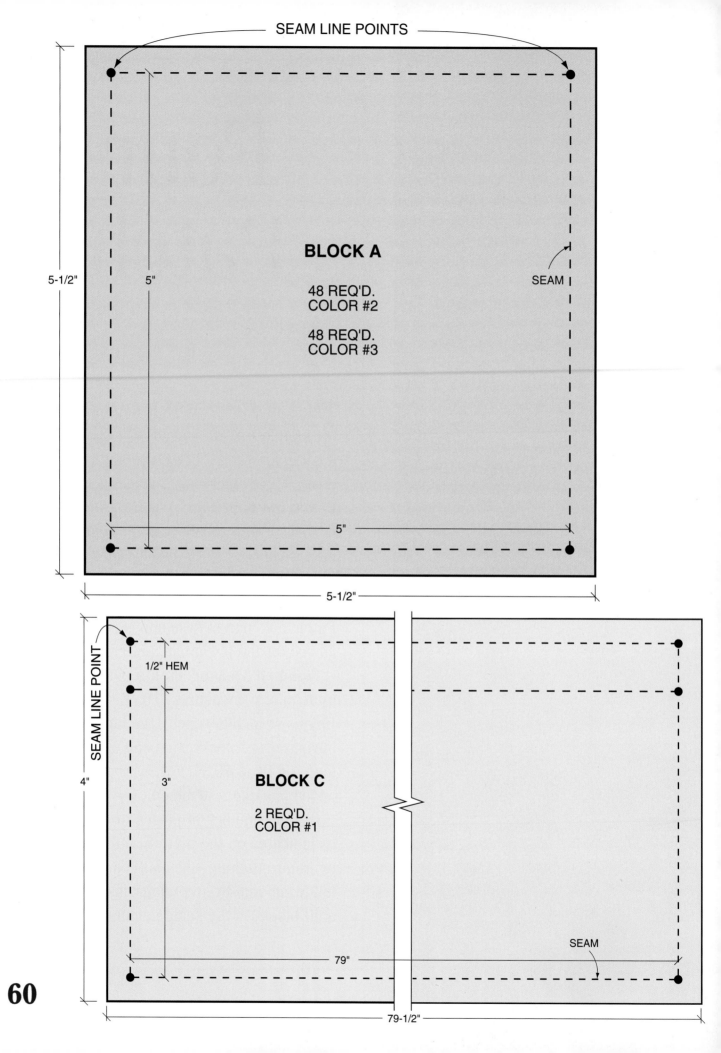

SEAM LINE POINTS

BLOCK A

48 REQ'D.
COLOR #2

48 REQ'D.
COLOR #3

SEAM

5-1/2"

5"

5"

5-1/2"

SEAM LINE POINT

1/2" HEM

3"

4"

BLOCK C

2 REQ'D.
COLOR #1

79"

SEAM

79-1/2"

60

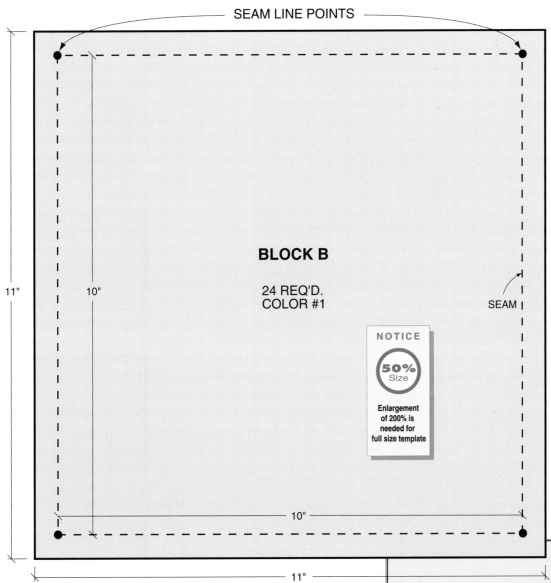

BLOCK B

24 REQ'D.
COLOR #1

NOTICE

50%
Size

Enlargement
of 200% is
needed for
full size template

11"

10"

10"

11"

SEAM

A #3

A #2

A #2

A #3

FULL QUILT BLOCK

Stitch the blocks together by rows, alternating the Four Patch blocks with plain blocks. Pin corners first, followed by the seams. Then, stitch with short running stitches. Join the finished rows two at a time, making sure to alternate rows to create a checkerboard effect. Be sure to match vertical seams before sewing.

Finishing: Add borders to edges and quilt or tie according to personal preference. Turn under hem all around, or bind edges as desired.

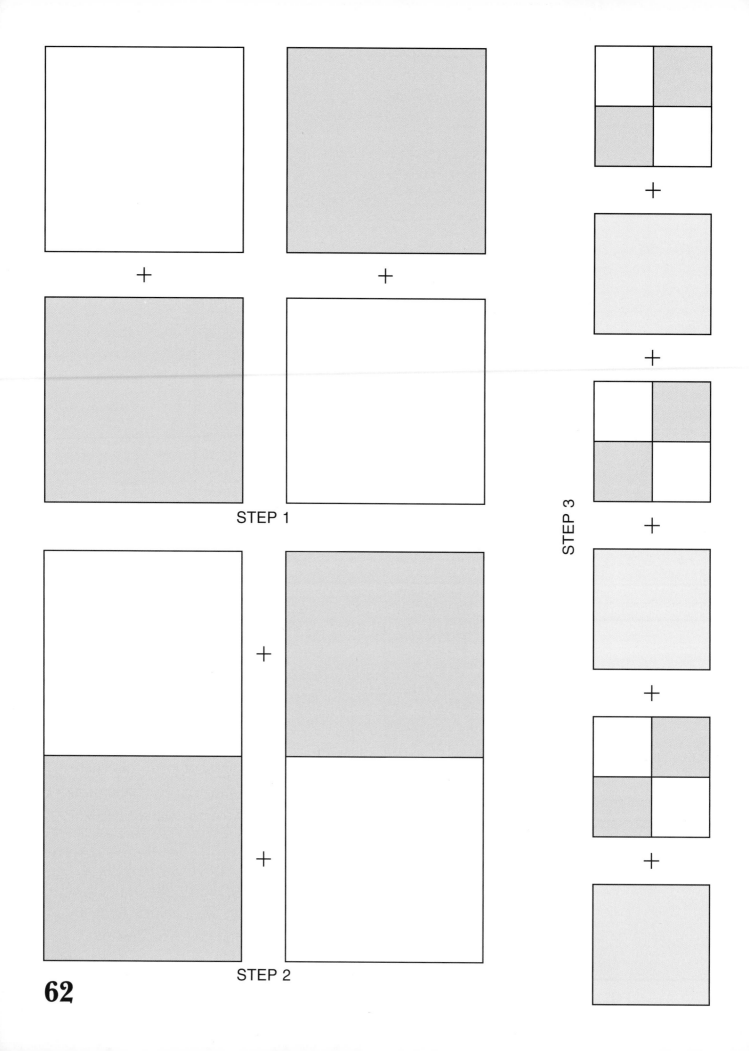

STEP 1

STEP 2

STEP 3

62

C

C

Nine Patch

This basic three-by-three grid has been a staple of American quilting since the early 1800's. The Nine Patch pattern provides the simplicity needed for a beginner, while offering unlimited variation potential for the advanced quilter. Simply altering piece sizes or dividing squares into triangles can open new creative avenues to the imaginative quilter. Further variations can be accomplished through the addition of sashing or by setting blocks at an angle. The possibilities truly are endless.

Finished Measurements: One finished quilt block measures 9 x 9 inches (minus seam allowance); the finished quilt measures seven blocks wide and nine blocks long, or 63 x 81 inches (minus edging).

Cut the number of pieces of each color as indicated on the pattern. Start machine or hand stitching the quilt block pieces, following the step-by-step diagrams. Alternate color pieces as indicated. Make

A #2	A #3	A #2				A #2	A #3	A #2
A #3	A #2	A #3		B #1		A #3	A #2	A #3
A #2	A #3	A #2				A #2	A #3	A #2
			A #2	A #3	A #2			
	B #1		A #3	A #2	A #3		B #1	
			A #2	A #3	A #2			
A #2	A #3	A #2				A #2	A #3	A #2
A #3	A #2	A #3		B #1		A #3	A #2	A #3
A #2	A #3	A #2				A #2	A #3	A #2

FULL QUILT BLOCK

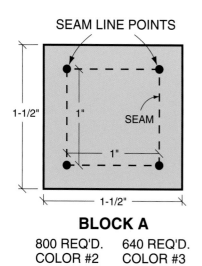

BLOCK A

800 REQ'D.   640 REQ'D.
COLOR #2   COLOR #3

SEAM LINE POINTS

1-1/2"

1"

SEAM

1"

1-1/2"

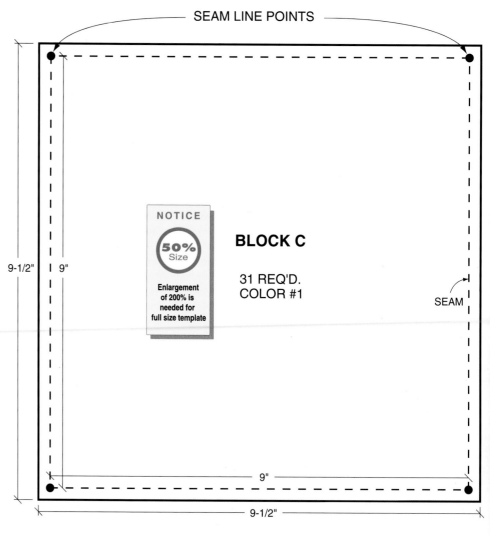

SEAM LINE POINTS

NOTICE

50% Size

Enlargement of 200% is needed for full size template

BLOCK C

31 REQ'D.
COLOR #1

SEAM

9-1/2"   9"

9"

9-1/2"

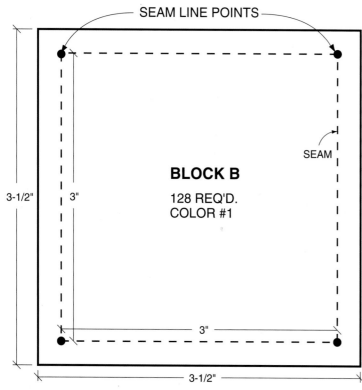

SEAM LINE POINTS

SEAM

BLOCK B

128 REQ'D.
COLOR #1

3-1/2"   3"

3"

3-1/2"

32 quilt blocks in the same manner.

Stitch the blocks together by rows, alternating pieced blocks with plain, as indicated. Pin corners first, followed by seams, then stitch with short running stitches. Join finished rows two at a time, matching vertical seams before sewing.

Finishing: Quilt or tie as to personal preference. Add desired binding to edges of completed quilt.

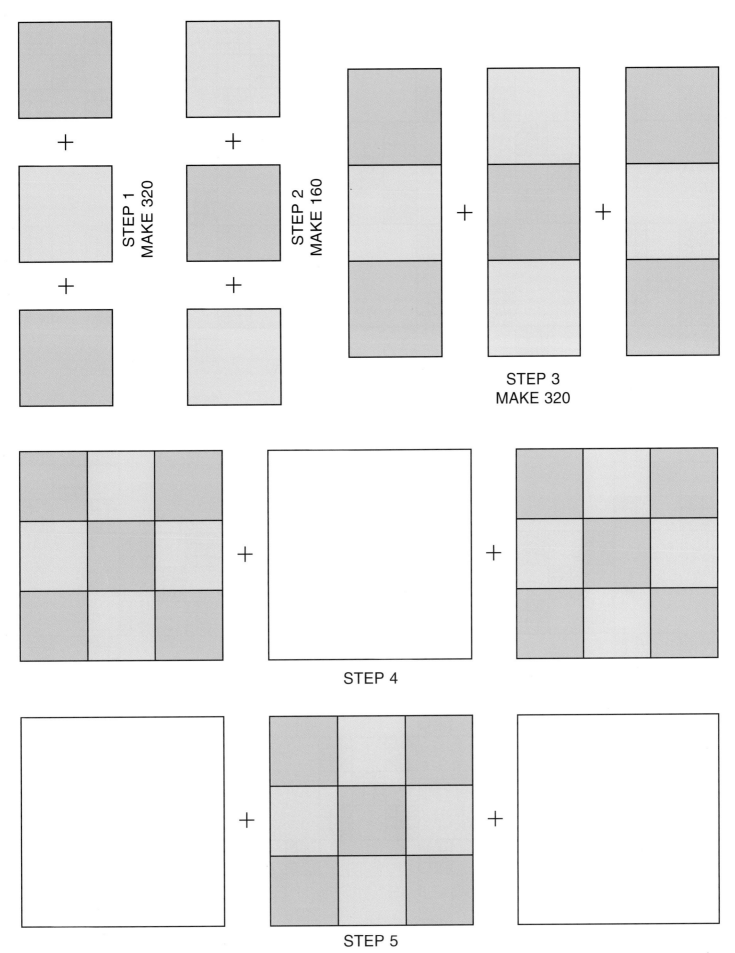

STEP 1
MAKE 320

STEP 2
MAKE 160

STEP 3
MAKE 320

STEP 4

STEP 5

67

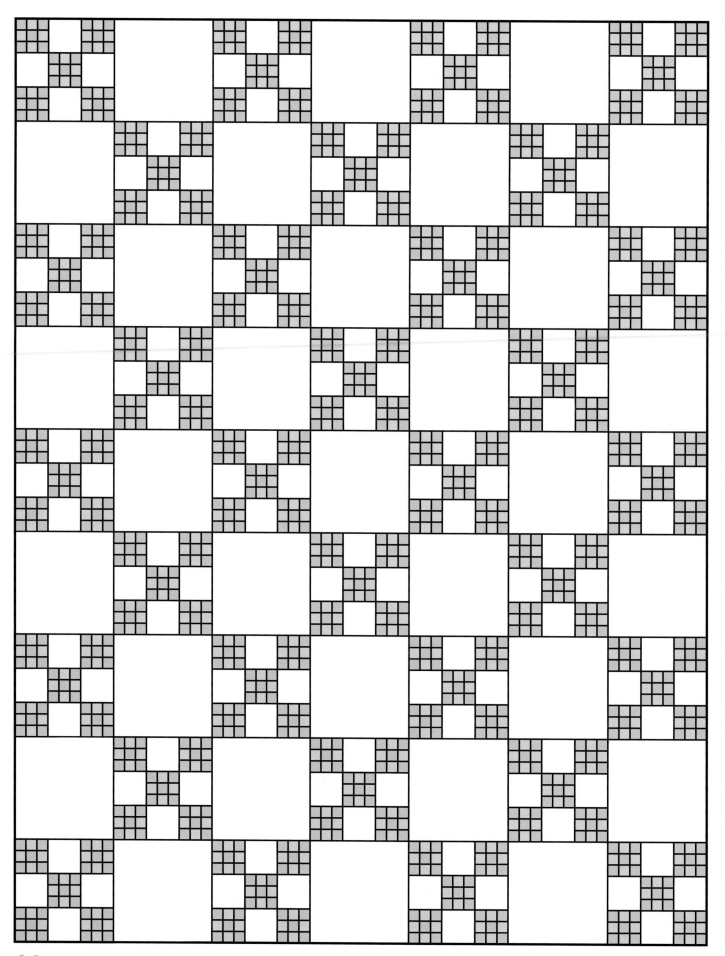

68

KALEIDOSCOPE

As its name suggests, this quilt block pattern is reminiscent of the mirrors and prisms of a kaleidoscope. Formed from squares and triangles, the pattern creates facets and diamonds. When pieced in shades of purple and lavender this quilt pattern is sometimes referred to as the Amethyst Quilt.

Although the Kaleidoscope pattern has several pieces, it is fairly easy to assemble. The asymmetrical block set may look difficult, but with careful attention to assembly it is easily demystified.

Finished Measurements: One finished *star* block measures 6-1/2 x 6-1/2 inches (minus seam allowance); the finished quilt measures seven blocks wide and seven blocks long, or 68 x 72-1/2 inches after border is added (minus edging).

Cut the number of pieces of each color as indicated on the pattern. Start machine or hand stitching the quilt block pieces, following the step-by-step diagrams and matching seam points to assure accuracy.

FULL QUILT BLOCK

D #2

C #1   C #1

D #2   B #2   D #2

C #1   C #1

D #2

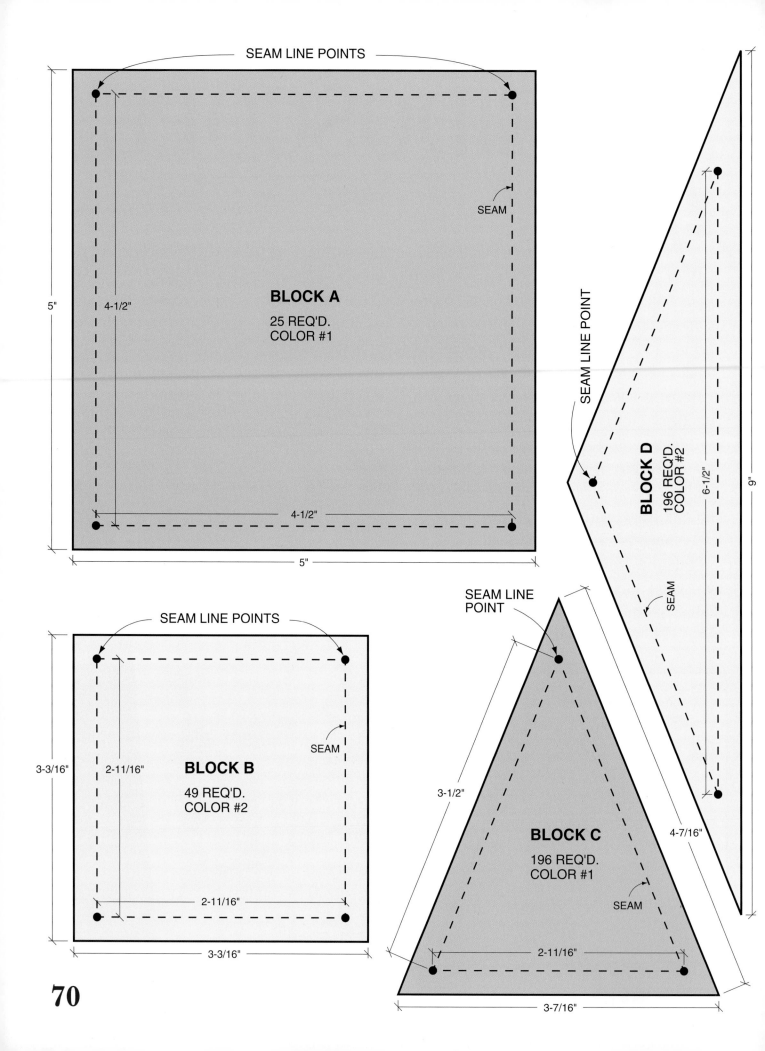

SEAM LINE POINTS

SEAM

BLOCK A

25 REQ'D.
COLOR #1

5"

4-1/2"

4-1/2"

5"

SEAM LINE POINT

SEAM

BLOCK D

196 REQ'D.
COLOR #2

6-1/2"

9"

4-7/16"

SEAM LINE POINTS

SEAM

BLOCK B

49 REQ'D.
COLOR #2

3-3/16"

2-11/16"

2-11/16"

3-3/16"

SEAM LINE
POINT

SEAM

BLOCK C

196 REQ'D.
COLOR #1

3-1/2"

2-11/16"

3-7/16"

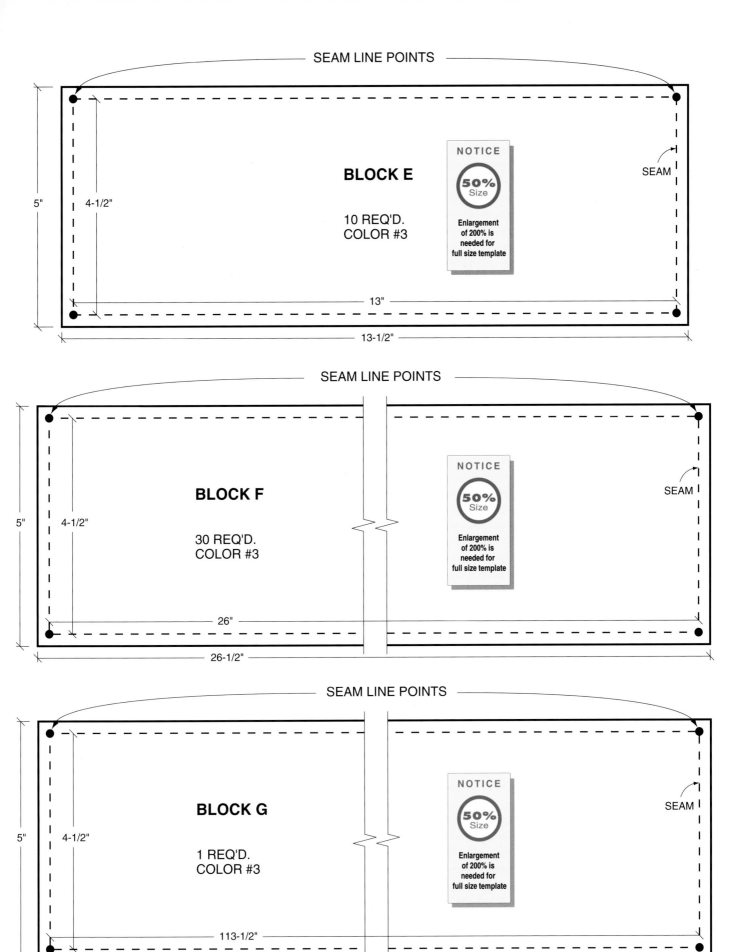

SEAM LINE POINTS

BLOCK E

10 REQ'D.
COLOR #3

NOTICE
50% Size
Enlargement of 200% is needed for full size template

SEAM

5"
4-1/2"
13"
13-1/2"

SEAM LINE POINTS

BLOCK F

30 REQ'D.
COLOR #3

NOTICE
50% Size
Enlargement of 200% is needed for full size template

SEAM

5"
4-1/2"
26"
26-1/2"

SEAM LINE POINTS

BLOCK G

1 REQ'D.
COLOR #3

NOTICE
50% Size
Enlargement of 200% is needed for full size template

SEAM

5"
4-1/2"
113-1/2"
114"

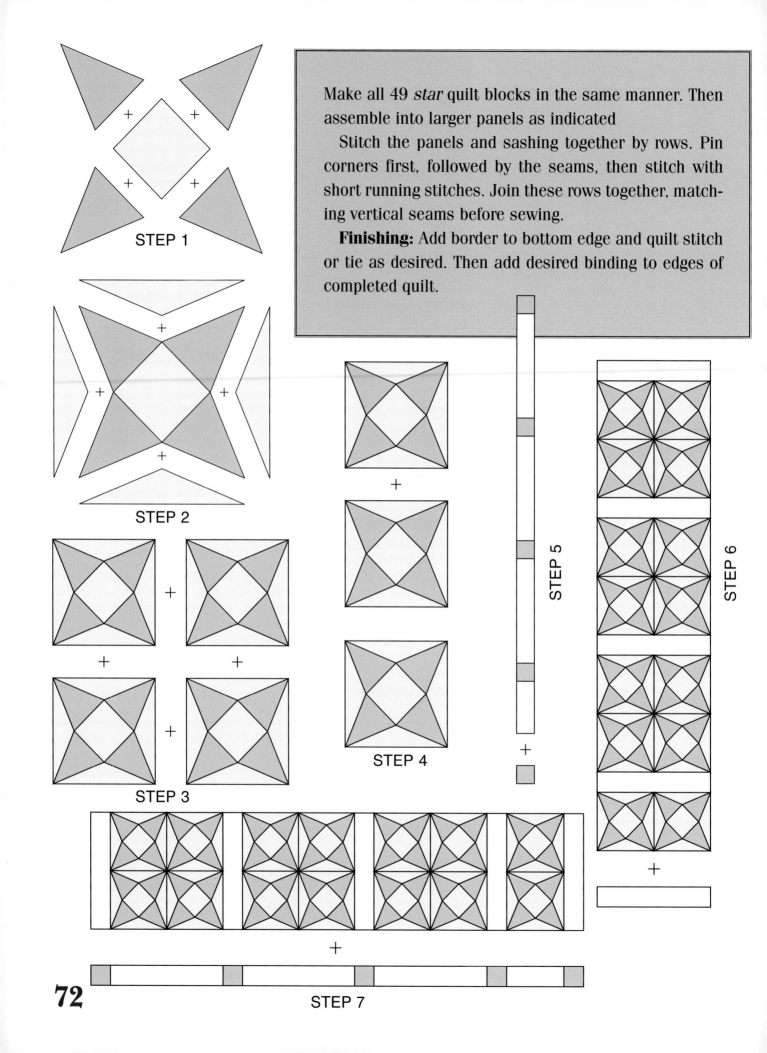

STEP 1

STEP 2

STEP 3

STEP 4

STEP 5

STEP 6

STEP 7

Make all 49 *star* quilt blocks in the same manner. Then assemble into larger panels as indicated

Stitch the panels and sashing together by rows. Pin corners first, followed by the seams, then stitch with short running stitches. Join these rows together, matching vertical seams before sewing.

Finishing: Add border to bottom edge and quilt stitch or tie as desired. Then add desired binding to edges of completed quilt.

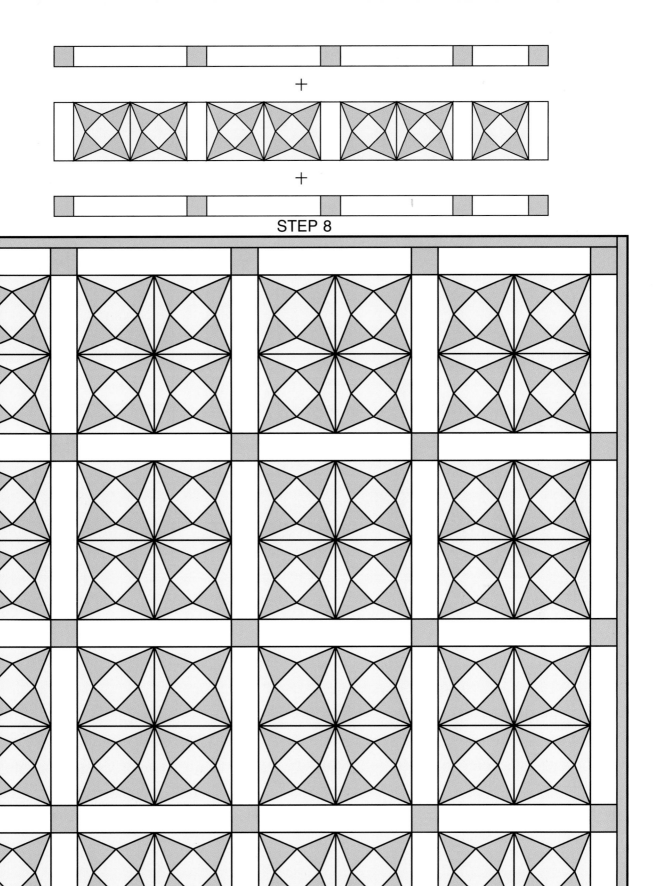

+

+

STEP 8

G

73

Churn Dash

Generally considered an old standard, there are several variations of this Nine Patch pattern. In some versions, the corner triangles are enlarged, or there are no rectangle pieces, yet the pattern names are repeated.

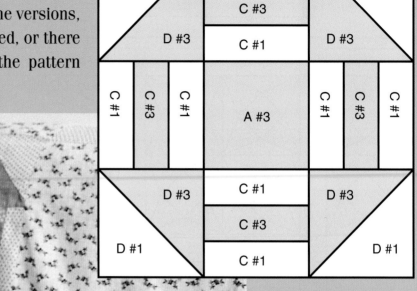

Likewise, the names of these related patterns are numerous. Primarily named after household items, this quilt pattern is also known as Wrench, Shoo Fly and Monkey Wrench. One name even has the historical reference, Sherman's March. All these names refer to a general group of Nine Patch patterns, which are most commonly called Churn Dash.

Finished Measurements: One finished quilt block measures 9 x 9 inches (minus seam allowance); finished quilt measures six blocks wide and seven blocks long, or 63 x 63 inches (minus edging) after borders are added.

Cut the number of pieces of each color as indicated on the pattern. Start machine or hand stitching quilt block pieces, following the step-by-step diagrams. Make 21 quilt blocks in the same manner.

Stitch the blocks together by rows, alternating pieced and plain blocks. Pin corners first, followed by the seams, then stitch using short running stitches. Join finished rows two at a time, matching vertical seams before sewing. Cut the remaining row in half horizontally, forming two *half rows*. Stitch one *half row* to the top and one *half row* to the bottom of the quilt top. Then sew borders to right and left sides of quilt.

Finishing: Quilt stitch or tie according to personal preference. Then, add desired binding to the edges of completed quilt.

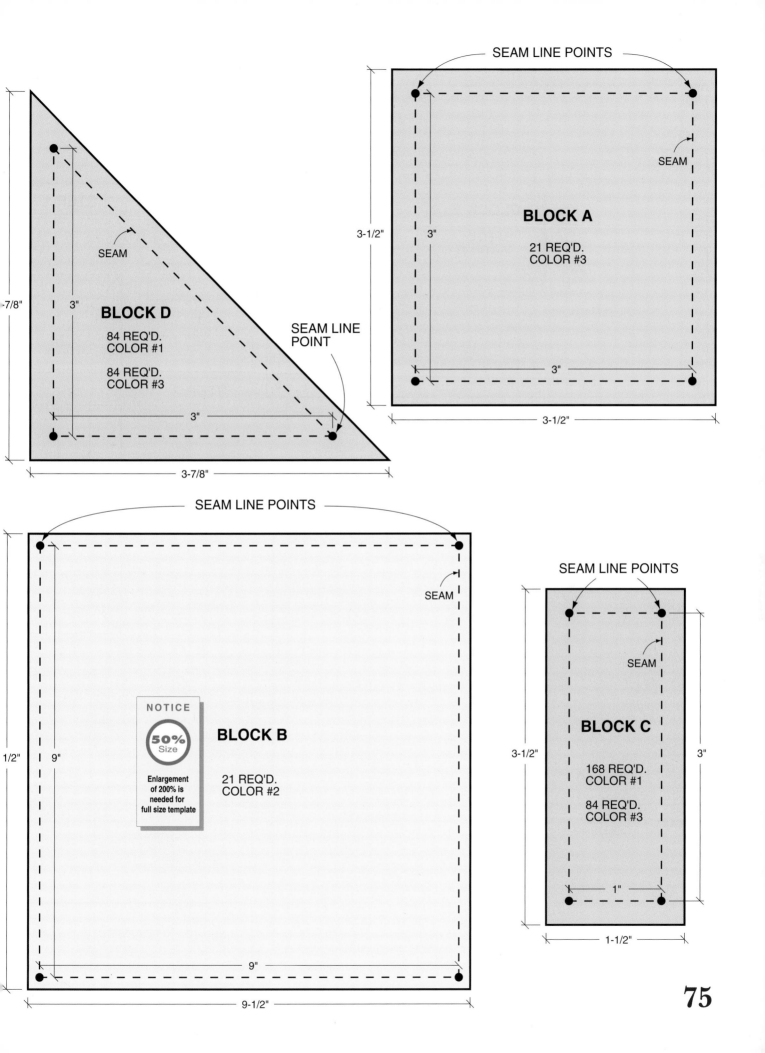

BLOCK D

84 REQ'D.
COLOR #1

84 REQ'D.
COLOR #3

SEAM

3"

3"

3-7/8"

3-7/8"

SEAM LINE
POINT

SEAM LINE POINTS

BLOCK A

21 REQ'D.
COLOR #3

SEAM

3-1/2"

3"

3"

3-1/2"

SEAM LINE POINTS

SEAM

BLOCK B

NOTICE

50% Size

Enlargement
of 200% is
needed for
full size template

21 REQ'D.
COLOR #2

9"

1/2"

9"

9-1/2"

SEAM LINE POINTS

SEAM

BLOCK C

168 REQ'D.
COLOR #1

84 REQ'D.
COLOR #3

3-1/2"

3"

1"

1-1/2"

75

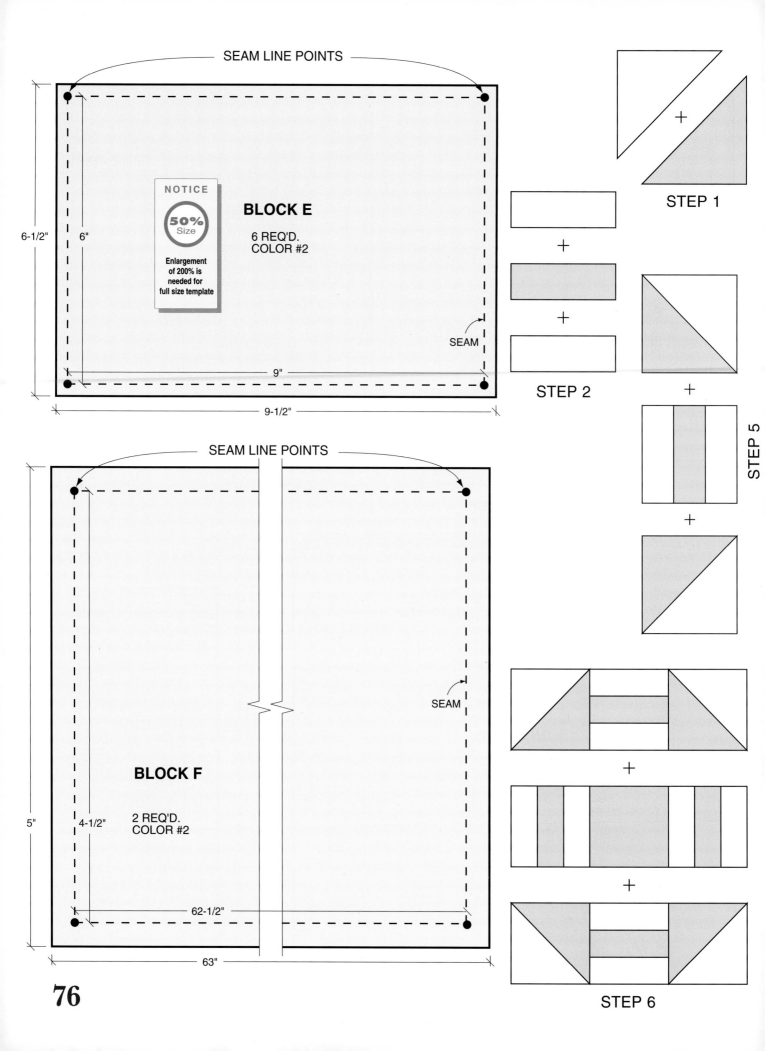

SEAM LINE POINTS

NOTICE

50% Size

Enlargement of 200% is needed for full size template

BLOCK E

6 REQ'D.
COLOR #2

6-1/2"

6"

9"

9-1/2"

SEAM

STEP 1

+

STEP 2

+

STEP 5

+

+

+

SEAM LINE POINTS

BLOCK F

2 REQ'D.
COLOR #2

5"

4-1/2"

62-1/2"

63"

SEAM

+

+

STEP 6

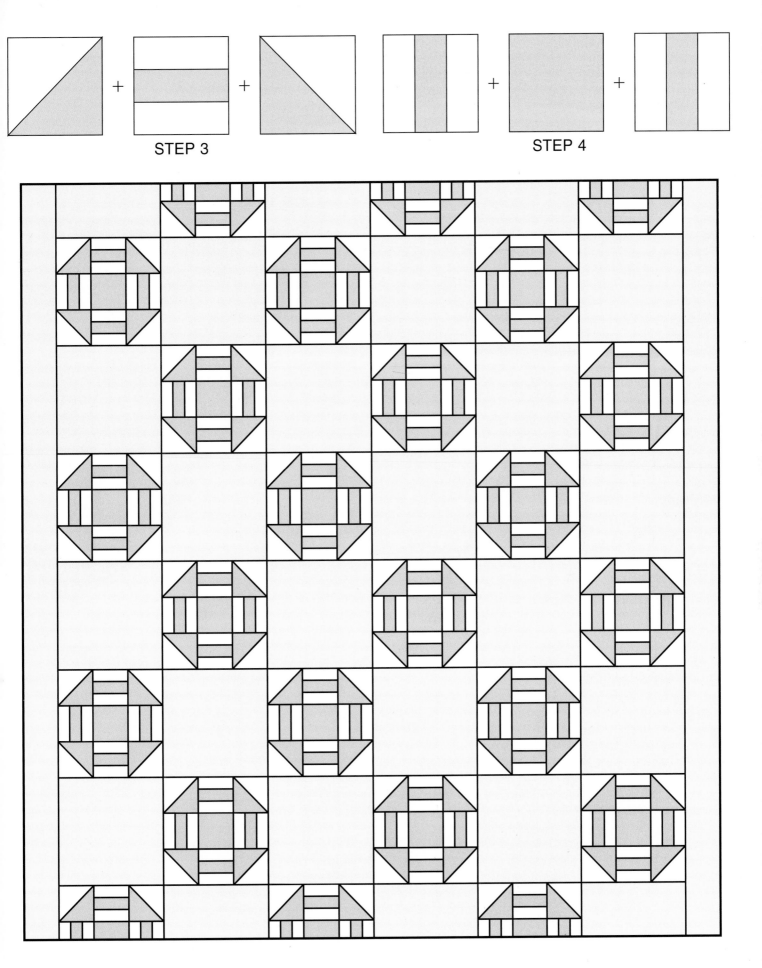

STEP 3

STEP 4

77

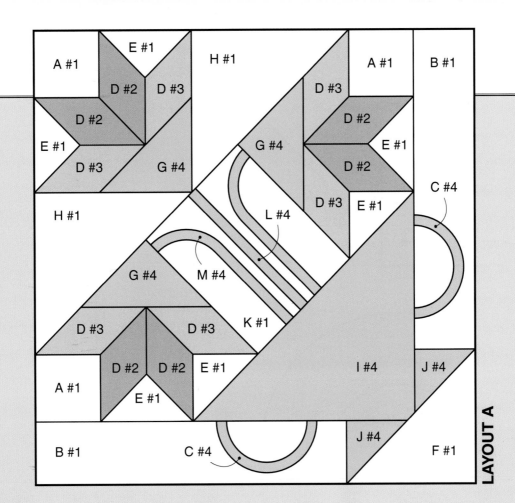

Basket of Lilies

This complex quilt block pattern, based on the LeMoyne Star, combines both piecing and appliqué methods. While the majority of the quilt is of the pieced style, the flower stems and the basket handles are appliquéed.

The early American pioneers, many of whom came to America to escape religious persecution, often incorporated their beliefs into everyday life. Thus, the Basket of Lilies pattern is rich with religious symbolism. The lily, a common symbol in Christianity, renders even greater significance when presented in a bouquet of three.

Finished Measurement: One finished quilt block measures 11 x 11 inches (minus seam allowance); the finished quilt is diagonally set and measures 70 x 81 inches (minus edging).

Cut the number of pieces of each color as indicated on the pattern. Start machine

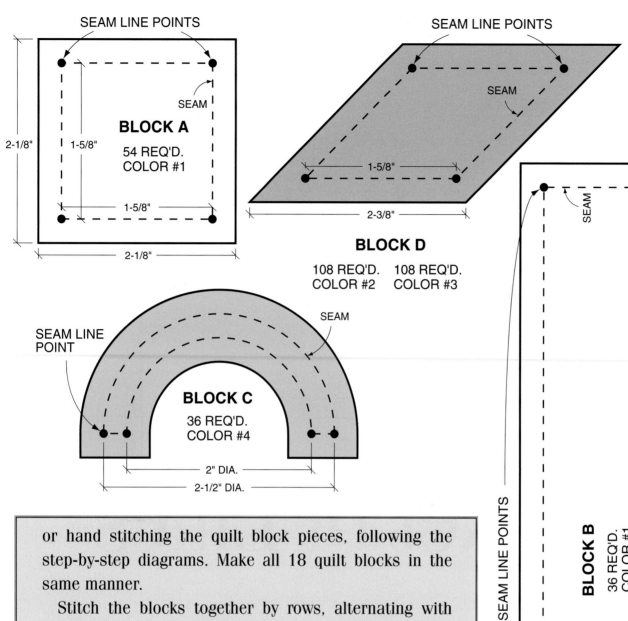

SEAM LINE POINTS

SEAM

BLOCK A

54 REQ'D.
COLOR #1

2-1/8"

1-5/8"

1-5/8"

2-1/8"

SEAM LINE POINTS

SEAM

BLOCK D

108 REQ'D.   108 REQ'D.
COLOR #2   COLOR #3

1-5/8"

2-3/8"

SEAM LINE
POINT

SEAM

BLOCK C

36 REQ'D.
COLOR #4

2" DIA.

2-1/2" DIA.

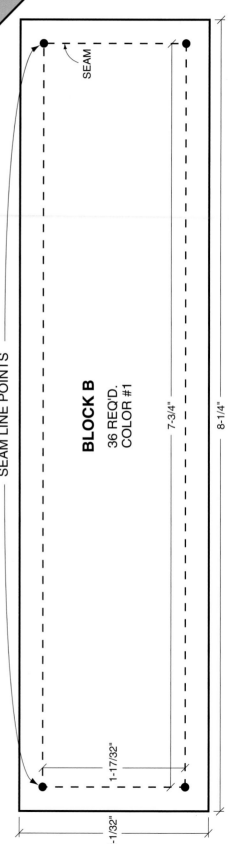

SEAM LINE POINTS

SEAM

BLOCK B

36 REQ'D.
COLOR #1

8-1/4"

7-3/4"

1-17/32"

2-1/32"

or hand stitching the quilt block pieces, following the step-by-step diagrams. Make all 18 quilt blocks in the same manner.

Stitch the blocks together by rows, alternating with sashing pieces, according to the diagrams. Pin corners first, followed by seams, then stitch using short running stitches. The quilt is a diagonally set design, so some blocks will need to be cut to form the end pieces of each row. These partial blocks fill the spaces around the edges and create the overall rectangular shape of the quilt. Join each finished row with a row of sashing, then connect those rows. Apply Amish-style borders in alphabetic sequence, according to quilt diagram.

Finishing: Quilt stitch or tie, according to personal preference. Then, add desired binding to the edges of the completed quilt.

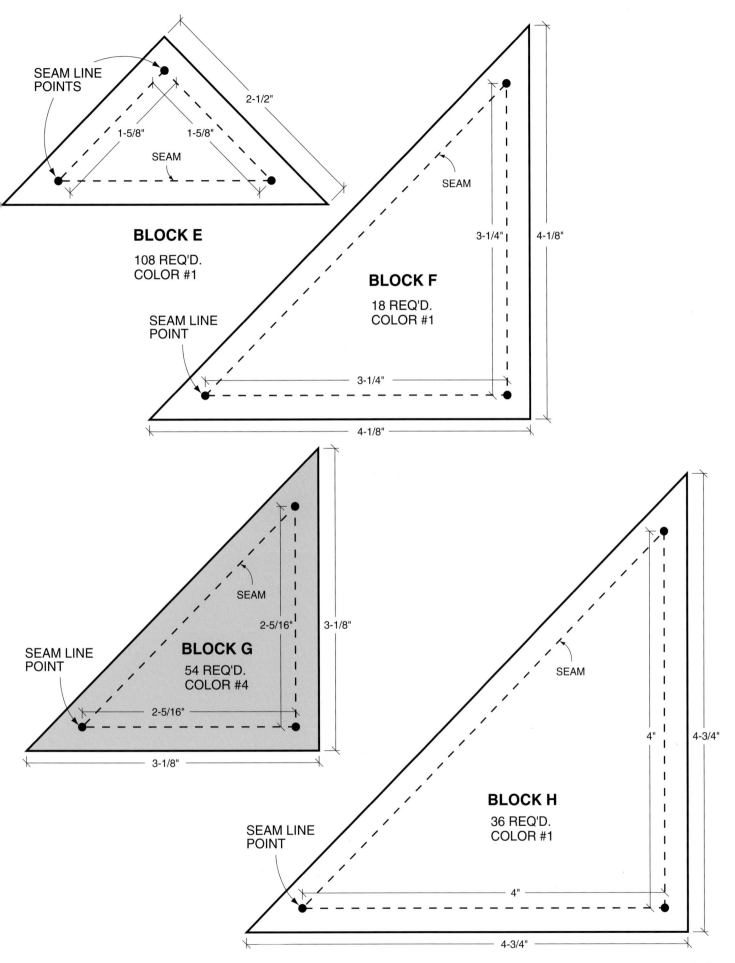

SEAM LINE
POINTS

2-1/2"

1-5/8"   1-5/8"

SEAM

BLOCK E

108 REQ'D.
COLOR #1

SEAM LINE
POINT

SEAM

3-1/4"   4-1/8"

BLOCK F

18 REQ'D.
COLOR #1

3-1/4"

4-1/8"

SEAM

2-5/16"   3-1/8"

SEAM LINE
POINT

BLOCK G

54 REQ'D.
COLOR #4

2-5/16"

3-1/8"

SEAM

4"   4-3/4"

SEAM LINE
POINT

BLOCK H

36 REQ'D.
COLOR #1

4"

4-3/4"

81

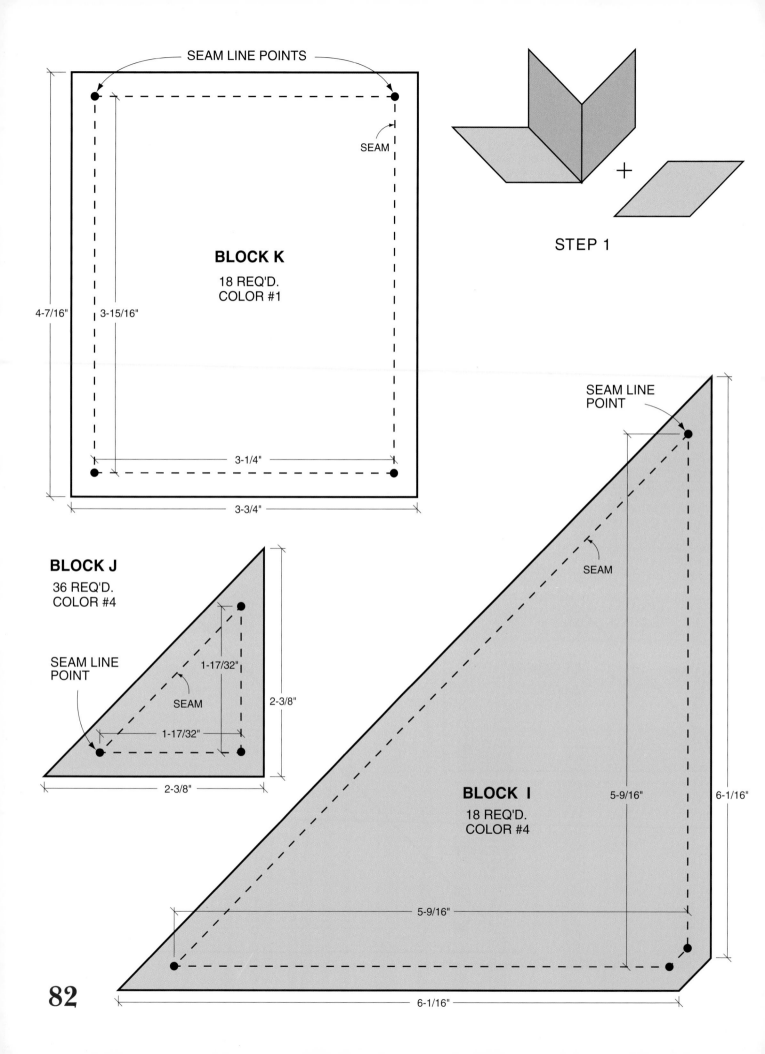

SEAM LINE POINTS

SEAM

BLOCK K

18 REQ'D.
COLOR #1

4-7/16"

3-15/16"

3-1/4"

3-3/4"

STEP 1

+

SEAM LINE
POINT

SEAM

BLOCK J

36 REQ'D.
COLOR #4

SEAM LINE
POINT

SEAM

1-17/32"

2-3/8"

1-17/32"

2-3/8"

BLOCK I

18 REQ'D.
COLOR #4

5-9/16"

6-1/16"

5-9/16"

6-1/16"

82

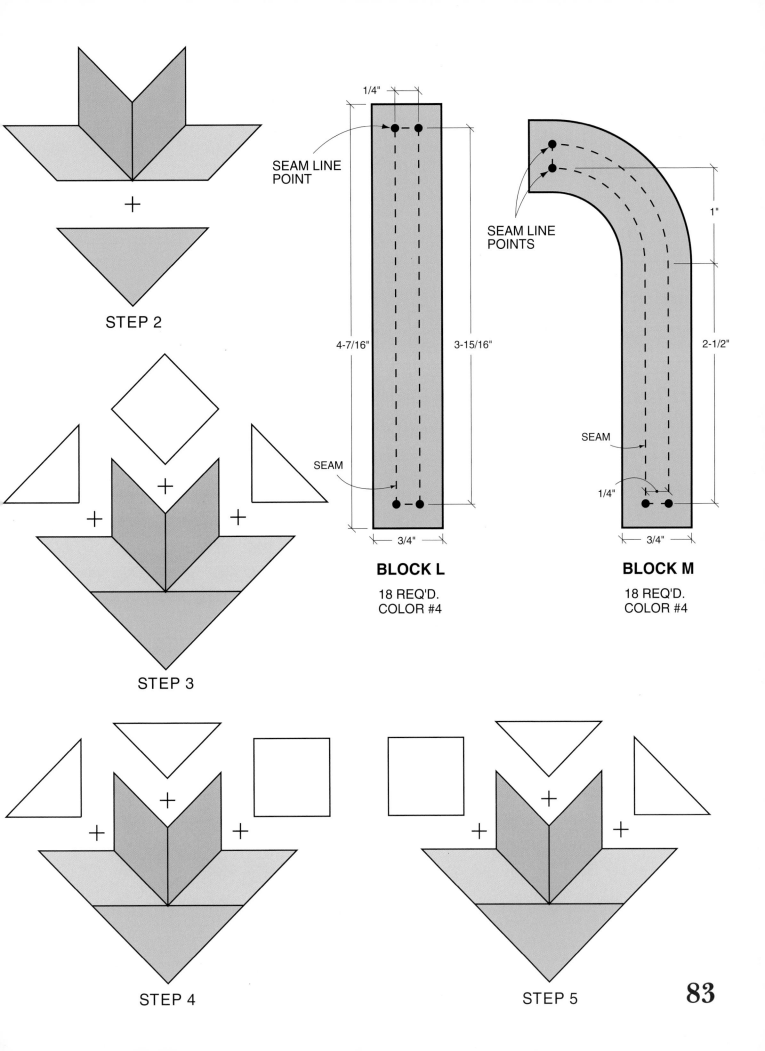

STEP 2

STEP 3

STEP 4

STEP 5

SEAM LINE
POINT

1/4"

4-7/16"

3-15/16"

SEAM

3/4"

BLOCK L

18 REQ'D.
COLOR #4

SEAM LINE
POINTS

1"

2-1/2"

SEAM

1/4"

3/4"

BLOCK M

18 REQ'D.
COLOR #4

83

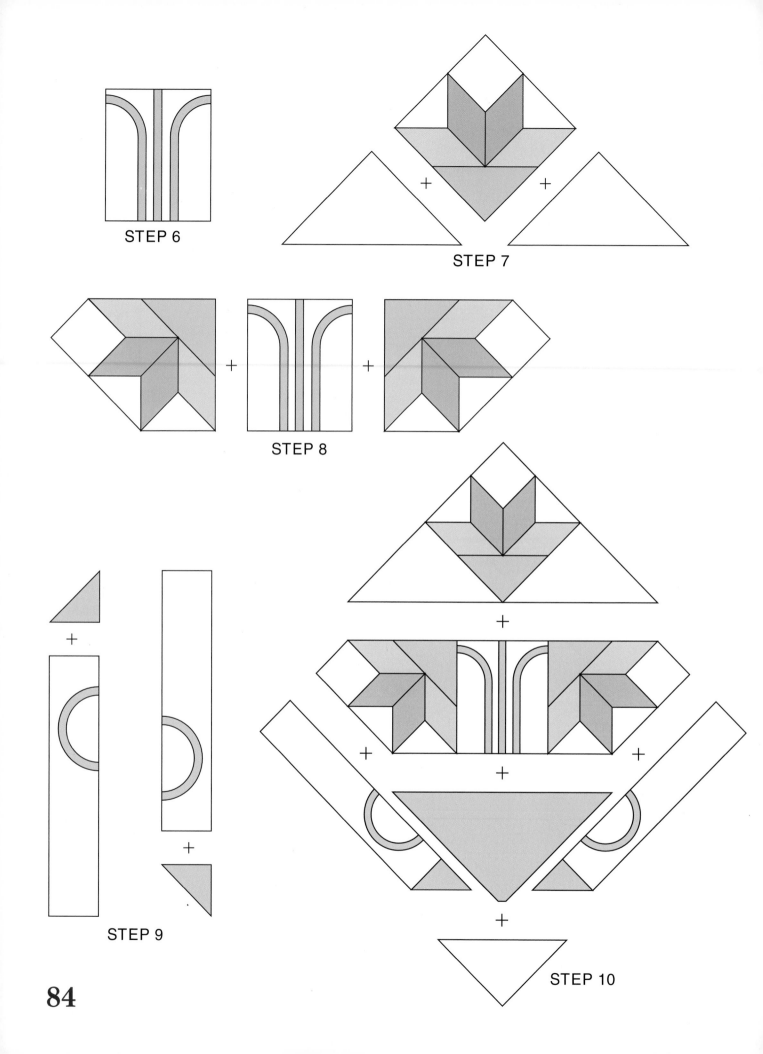

STEP 6

STEP 7

STEP 8

STEP 9

STEP 10

84

85

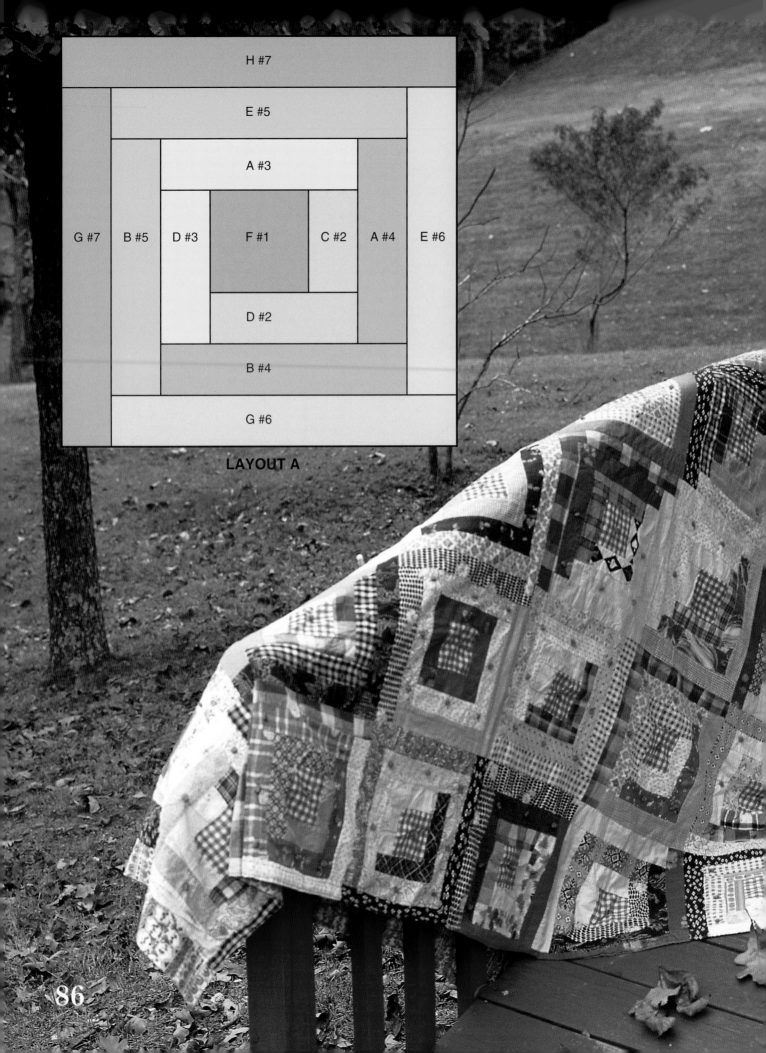

H #7

E #5

A #3

G #7 | B #5 | D #3 | F #1 | C #2 | A #4 | E #6

D #2

B #4

G #6

LAYOUT A

Log Cabin

Though many associate this quilt pattern with the early American pioneers, some quilt historians consider the methods used to be ancient. Egyptian mummies were found wrapped in a fabric that was assembled in a fashion quite similar to the Log Cabin quilt pattern. Others view this pattern as an English design from around the early 1800's.

Though these inconsistent claims of origin have caused controversy, it is certain that America's love affair with the Log Cabin design blossomed around the end of the 19th century. This block was, and remains, one of the most popular and widely used quilt patterns.

Perhaps as a result of such popularity, there appears to be nearly as many variations to this design as there are quilters. A traditional block has a center square of red or yellow fabric, symbolizing the hearth and home. During the era of slavery, this pattern was used surreptitiously by the Underground Railroad. A log cabin quilt with a black center block was the sign of a "safe haven" for fleeing slaves.

Finished Measurements: One finished quilt block measures 12 x 12 inches (minus seam allowance); the finished quilt measures six blocks wide and six blocks long, or 72 x 72 inches (minus edging).

Cut the number of pieces of each color as indicated on the pattern. Start machine or hand stitching the quilt block pieces, following the step-by-step diagrams. Make all 36 quilt blocks in the same manner.

Stitch the blocks together by rows. Pin corners first, followed by seams, then stitch with short running stitches. Join finished rows two at a time, matching vertical seams before sewing.

Finishing: Quilt stitch or tie quilt according to personal preference, Then, add desired binding to edges of completed quilt.

87

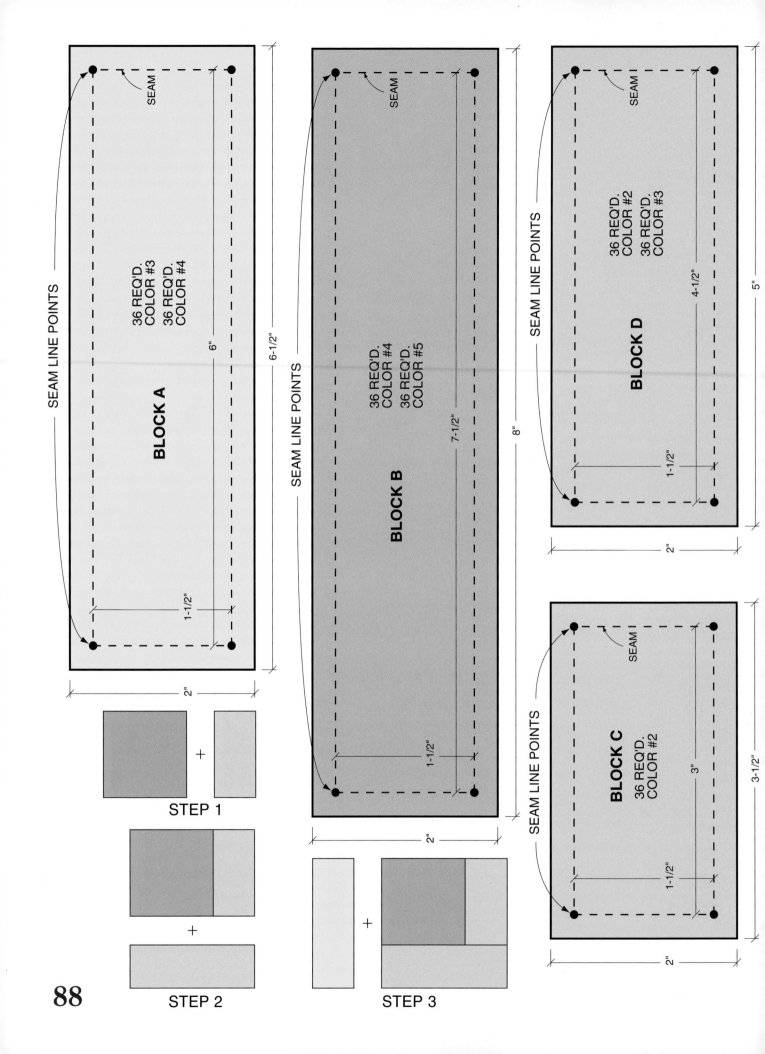

SEAM LINE POINTS

SEAM

BLOCK A

36 REQ'D.
COLOR #3
36 REQ'D.
COLOR #4

6"

6-1/2"

1-1/2"

2"

SEAM LINE POINTS

SEAM LINE POINTS

SEAM

BLOCK B

36 REQ'D.
COLOR #4
36 REQ'D.
COLOR #5

7-1/2"

8"

1-1/2"

2"

SEAM LINE POINTS

SEAM

BLOCK D

36 REQ'D.
COLOR #2
36 REQ'D.
COLOR #3

4-1/2"

5"

1-1/2"

2"

SEAM LINE POINTS

SEAM

BLOCK C

36 REQ'D.
COLOR #2

3"

3-1/2"

1-1/2"

2"

STEP 1

+

STEP 2

+

STEP 3

+

88

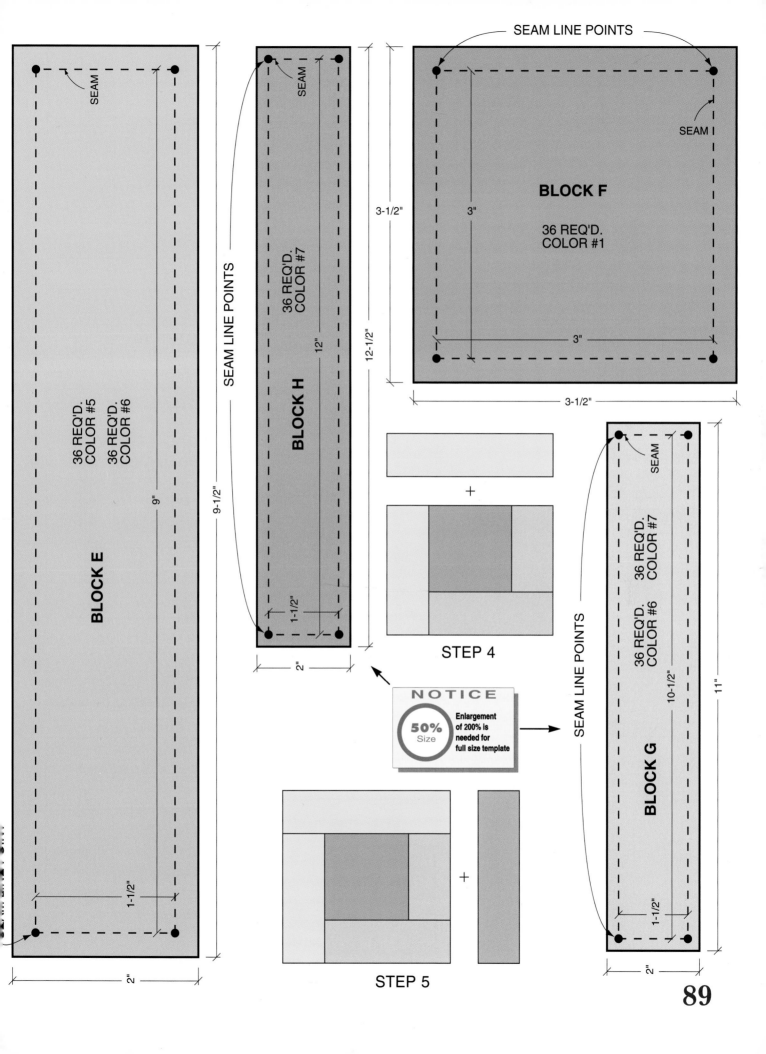

BLOCK E

36 REQ'D.
COLOR #5

36 REQ'D.
COLOR #6

SEAM

9"

9-1/2"

1-1/2"

2"

BLOCK H

36 REQ'D.
COLOR #7

SEAM

12"

1-1/2"

2"

SEAM LINE POINTS

SEAM LINE POINTS

12-1/2"

3-1/2"

BLOCK F

36 REQ'D.
COLOR #1

3"

3"

3-1/2"

SEAM

SEAM LINE POINTS

STEP 4

+

NOTICE

50% Size

Enlargement
of 200% is
needed for
full size template

BLOCK G

36 REQ'D.
COLOR #6

36 REQ'D.
COLOR #7

SEAM

10-1/2"

11"

1-1/2"

2"

SEAM LINE POINTS

STEP 5

+

89

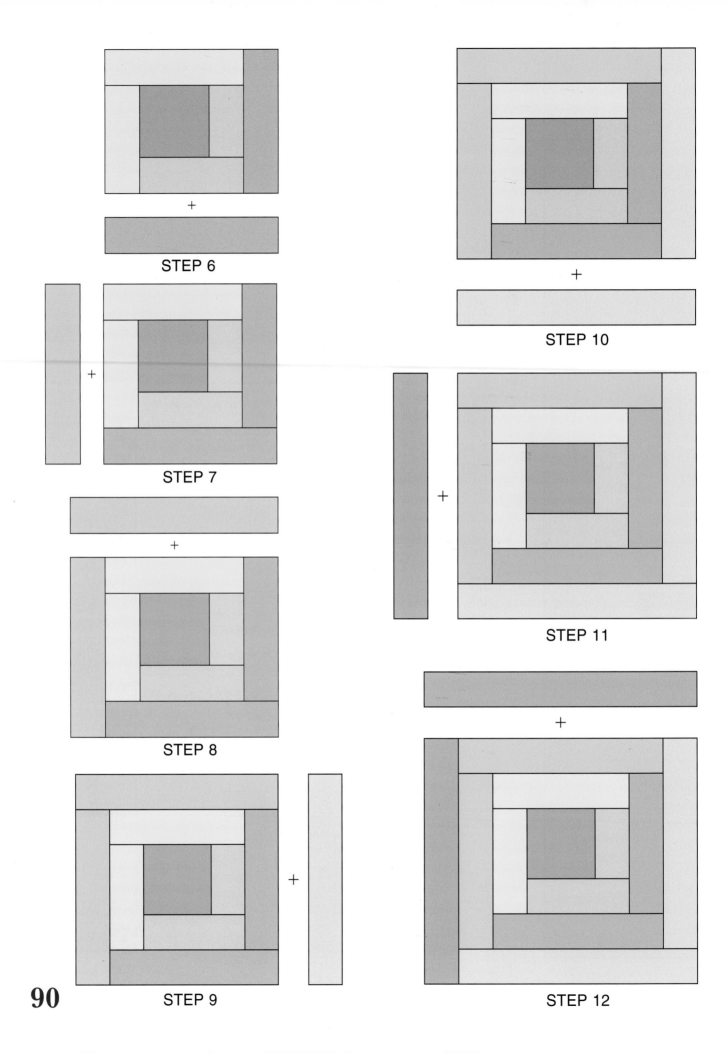

STEP 6

STEP 7

STEP 8

STEP 9

STEP 10

STEP 11

STEP 12

90

Diamond Quilt

Inspired by centuries old Near-Eastern tile work, the diamond was one of the first geometric shapes used in pieced quilting. Although often used as a key component for creating star patterns and other motifs, the diamond rarely shines alone in the spotlight. This quilt is an exception. With such bold use of color, the diamond gets all the recognition it deserves.

Finished Measurements: One finished diamond quilt block measures 7 x 13 inches (minus seam allowance); finished quilt measures 5-1/2 blocks wide

and 8-1/2 blocks long, or 75-3/4 x 81-1/2 inches with borders added (minus edging).

Cut the number of pieces of each color as indicated on the pattern. Start machine or hand stitching the quilt block pieces, following the step-by-step diagrams. Make 80 quilt blocks in the same manner. Make 16 half blocks as shown in Layout B; 10 half blocks as shown in Layout C; and two quarter blocks as shown in Layout D.

Stitch the blocks together by rows. Pin corners first, followed by the seams, then stitch with short running stitches. Join the finished rows two at a time, matching intersecting seams before sewing.

Add borders and corner squares as

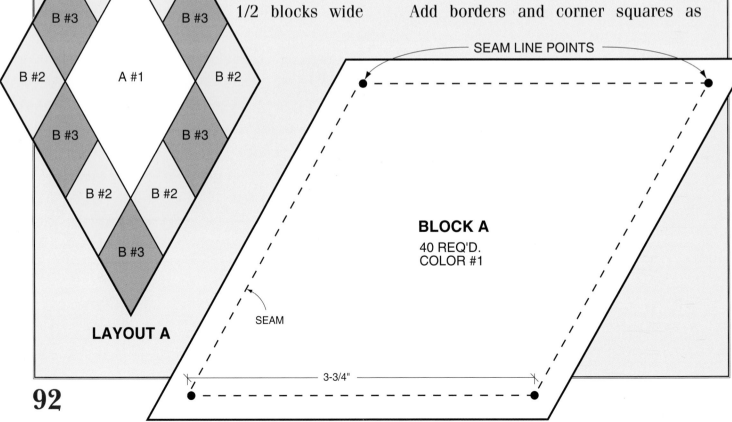

LAYOUT A

SEAM LINE POINTS

SEAM

BLOCK A
40 REQ'D.
COLOR #1

3-3/4"

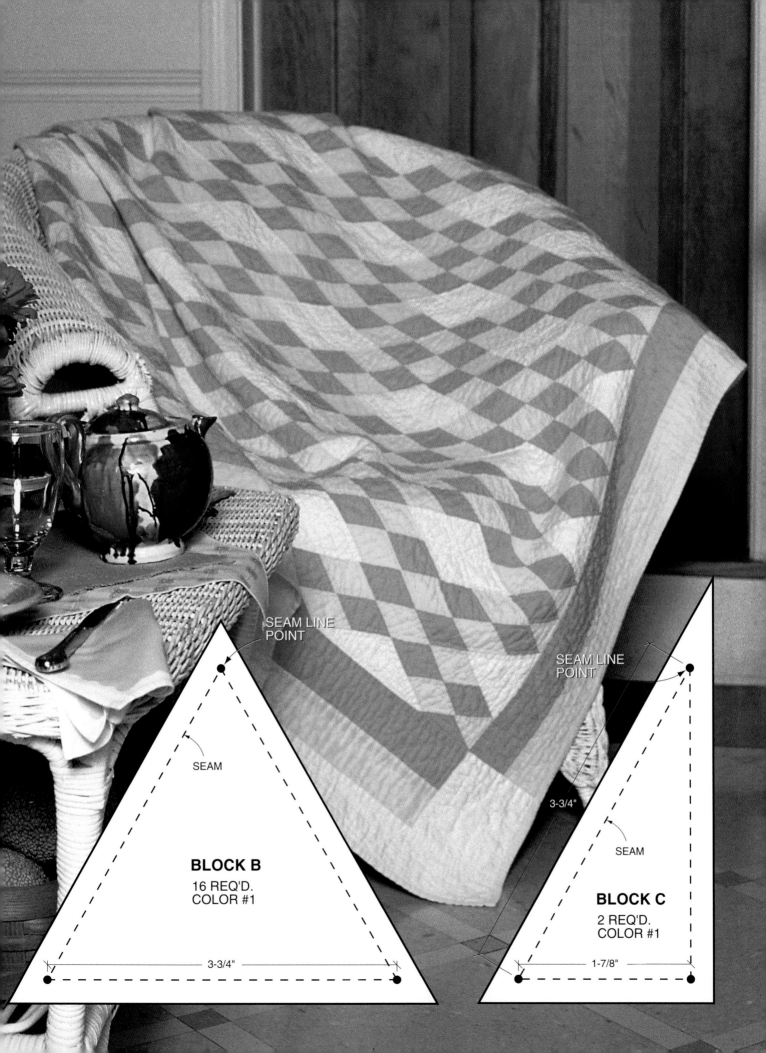

SEAM LINE POINT

SEAM

BLOCK B
16 REQ'D.
COLOR #1

3-3/4"

SEAM LINE POINT

3-3/4"

SEAM

BLOCK C
2 REQ'D.
COLOR #1

1-7/8"

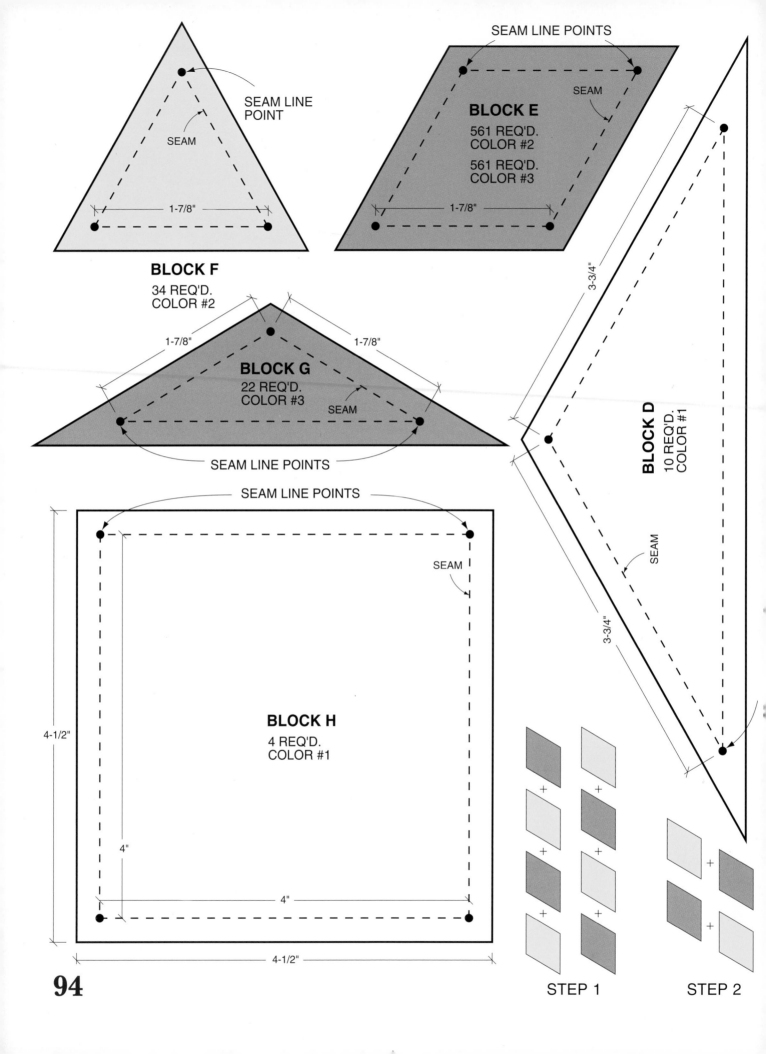

SEAM LINE POINTS

SEAM LINE
POINT

SEAM

BLOCK E

561 REQ'D.
COLOR #2

561 REQ'D.
COLOR #3

SEAM

1-7/8"

BLOCK F

34 REQ'D.
COLOR #2

1-7/8"

1-7/8"

1-7/8"

BLOCK G

22 REQ'D.
COLOR #3

SEAM

SEAM LINE POINTS

3-3/4"

BLOCK D

10 REQ'D.
COLOR #1

SEAM

3-3/4"

SEAM LINE POINTS

SEAM

4-1/2"

4"

BLOCK H

4 REQ'D.
COLOR #1

4"

4-1/2"

94

STEP 1

STEP 2

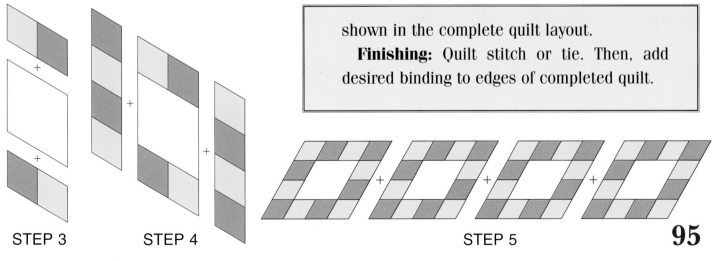

shown in the complete quilt layout.

Finishing: Quilt stitch or tie. Then, add desired binding to edges of completed quilt.

STEP 3   STEP 4   STEP 5   **95**

Fifty-Four-Forty Or Fight

Like many quilt blocks, this Nine-Patch quilt pattern carries a name that reflects the political turmoil of its time. Politically-inspired names for quilt patterns quickly identify the period of a quilt's popularity. The slogan "Fifty-Four-Forty or Fight" was used during the boundary dispute over the Oregon Territory, between the United States and Britain. This reference dates the pattern, or at least its naming, between 1830 and 1840.

Finished Measurements: One finished quilt block measures 9 x 9 inches (minus seam allowance); the finished quilt measures seven blocks wide and eight blocks long, or 63 x 72 inches (minus edging).

Cut the number of pieces of each color as indicated on the pattern. Start machine or hand stitching the quilt block pieces, following the step-by-step diagrams. Make 28 quilt blocks in the same manner.

Stitch blocks together by rows, alternating pieced squares with plain. Be sure to begin four rows with pieced blocks and four rows with plain. Pin corners first, followed by the seams, then stitch with short running stitches. Join finished rows two at a time, stitching a row with a pieced first block to a row having a plain first block. Be sure to match vertical seams before sewing.

Finishing: Quilt stitch or tie. Then, add desired binding to completed quilt.

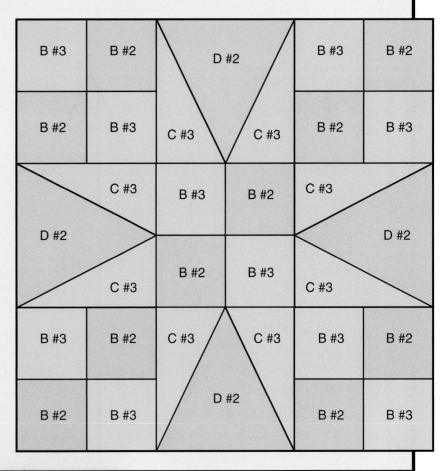

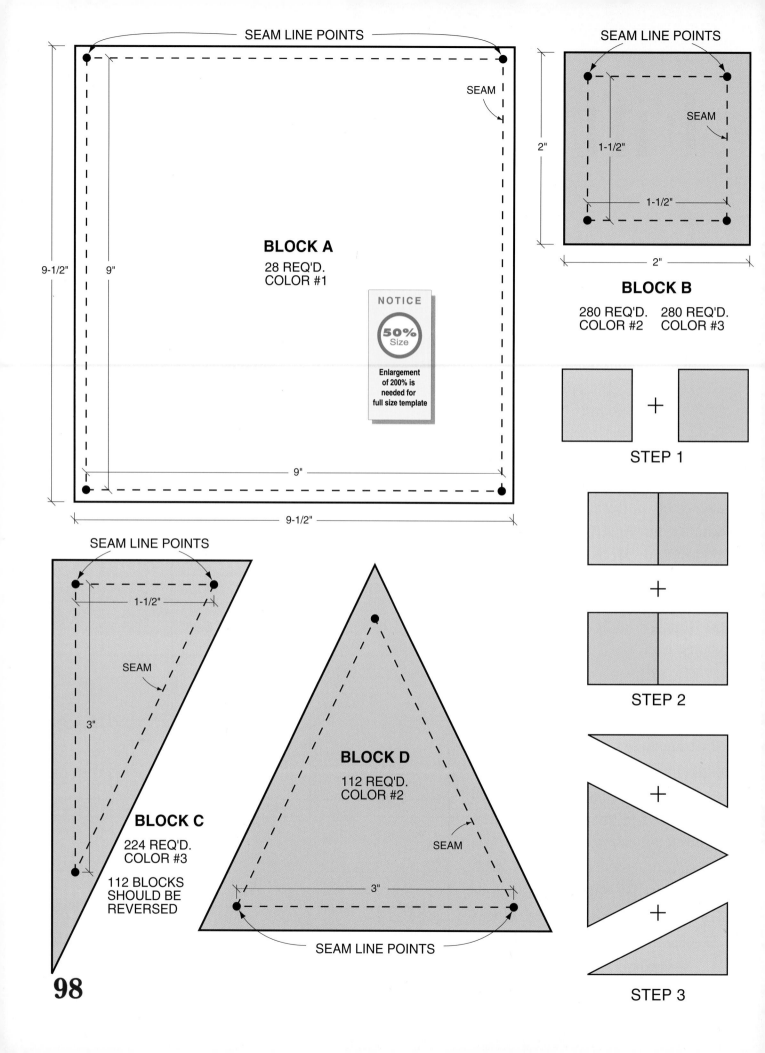

SEAM LINE POINTS

BLOCK A

28 REQ'D.
COLOR #1

NOTICE
50%
Size

Enlargement
of 200% is
needed for
full size template

SEAM

9-1/2"
9"
9"
9-1/2"

SEAM LINE POINTS

2"
1-1/2"
1-1/2"
2"

SEAM

BLOCK B

280 REQ'D.   280 REQ'D.
COLOR #2   COLOR #3

+

STEP 1

+

STEP 2

SEAM LINE POINTS

1-1/2"

SEAM

3"

BLOCK C

224 REQ'D.
COLOR #3

112 BLOCKS
SHOULD BE
REVERSED

BLOCK D

112 REQ'D.
COLOR #2

SEAM

3"

SEAM LINE POINTS

+

+

STEP 3

98

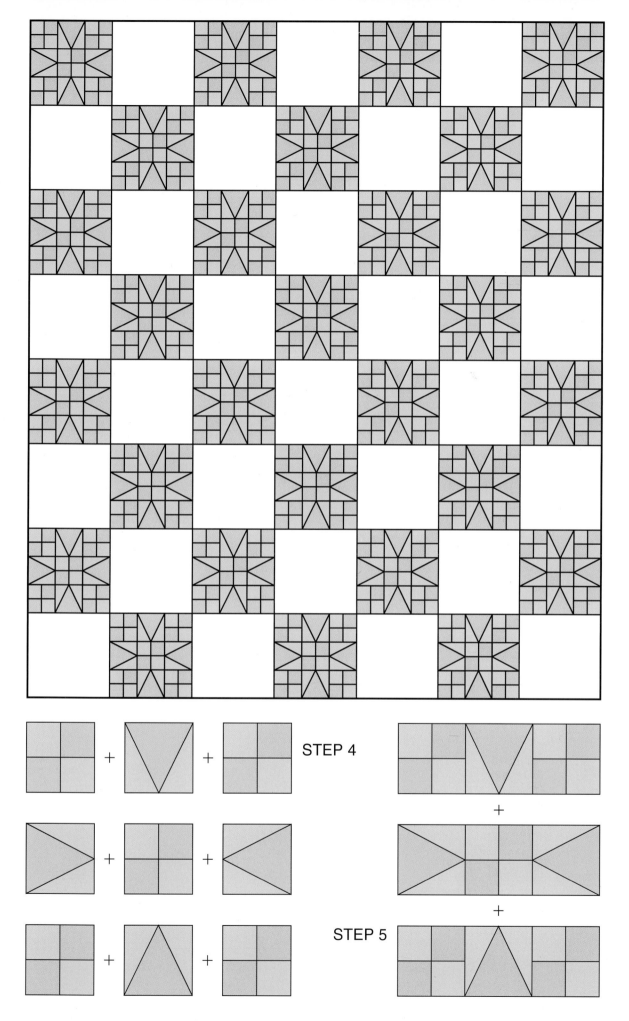

STEP 4

STEP 5

99

SEAM LINE POINTS

3"

2-1/2"

BLOCK A

25 REQ'D.
COLOR #3

SEAM

2-1/2"

3"

Bow Tie

*T*his charming quilt is based on a Four Patch design and was originally drawn on a 16 square grid. The pattern, as it appears here, is a simplified version of the very intricate original. Rest assured the finished result will look every bit as good worked in the easier Four Patch design.

You may see similar quilts called by other names, including Necktie, Colonial Bowtie and True Lover's Knot.

Finished Measurements: One finished quilt block measures 6 x 6 inches (minus seam allowance); finished quilt measures five blocks wide and five blocks long, or 47 x 47 inches (minus edging).

Cut the number of pieces of each color as indicated on the pattern. Start machine or hand stitching the quilt block pieces, following the step-by-step diagrams. Make all 25 quilt blocks in the same manner.

Stitch the blocks together by rows, adding sashing pieces between the blocks. Prepare four full rows of sashing. Then, join the resulting rows two at a time, matching vertical seams before sewing. Attach borders to quilt top.

Finishing: Quilt stitch or tie. Then, add desired binding to edges of completed quilt.

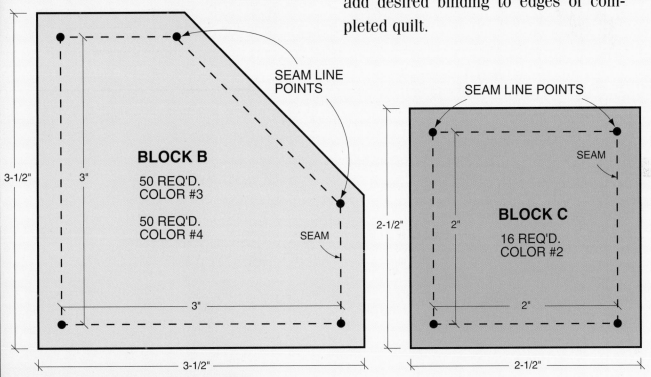

SEAM LINE POINTS

BLOCK B

50 REQ'D. COLOR #3

50 REQ'D. COLOR #4

SEAM

3-1/2"
3"
3"
3-1/2"

SEAM LINE POINTS

SEAM

BLOCK C

16 REQ'D. COLOR #2

2-1/2"
2"
2"
2-1/2"

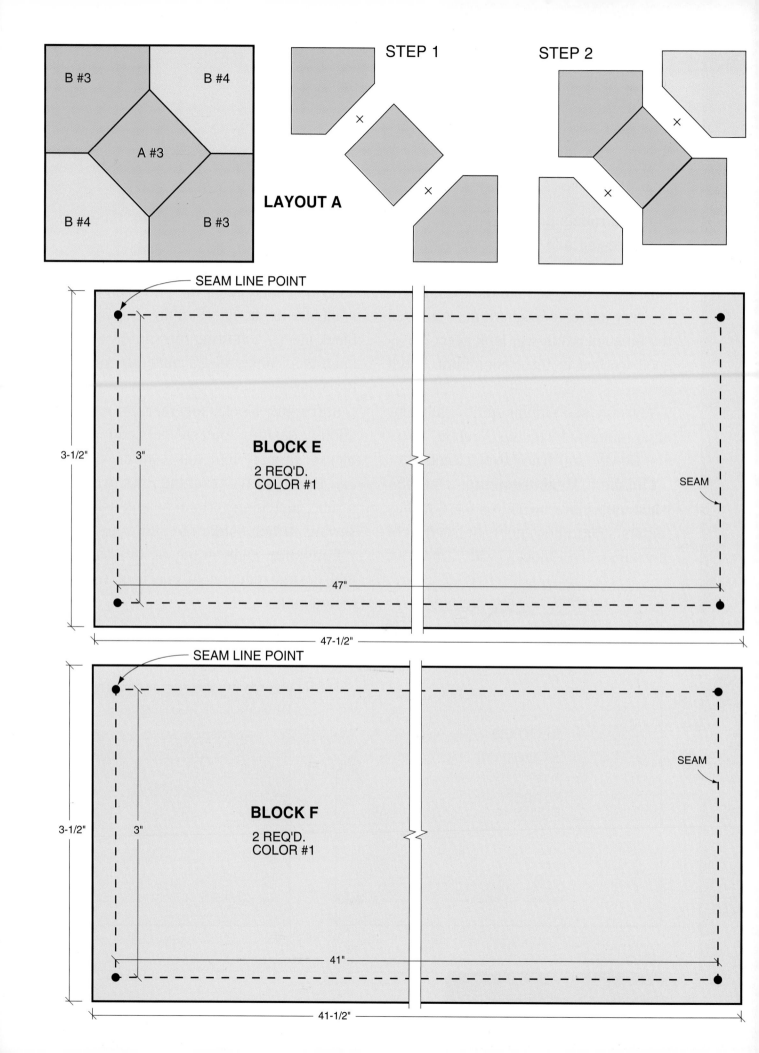

LAYOUT A

B #3   B #4

A #3

B #4   B #3

STEP 1

STEP 2

SEAM LINE POINT

BLOCK E

2 REQ'D.
COLOR #1

SEAM

3-1/2"

3"

47"

47-1/2"

SEAM LINE POINT

BLOCK F

2 REQ'D.
COLOR #1

SEAM

3-1/2"

3"

41"

41-1/2"

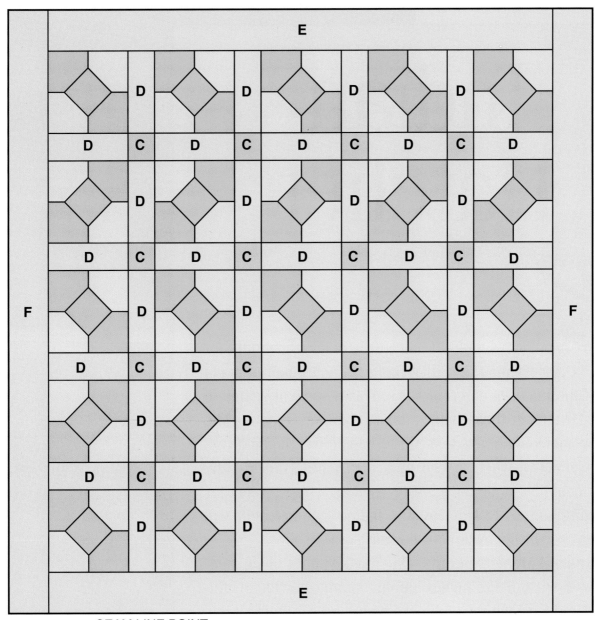

E

F   F

E

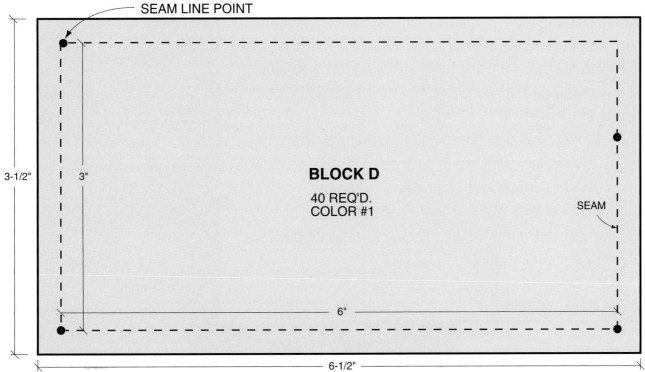

SEAM LINE POINT

3-1/2"   3"

BLOCK D

40 REQ'D.
COLOR #1

SEAM

6"

6-1/2"

103

Indian Hatchet

Based on a simple-to-piece little block, this quilt pattern is perfect for the novice quilter. Each block is made up of three pieces and requires only two straight seams to join. When set, these basic shapes combine, creating the impression of hatchets laid end-to-end across the quilt top. Most effective when pieced from contrasting fabrics, the quilt could be made for a gift or used as a first project for a young quilter. Either way, the Indian Hatchet quilt will delight the little cowboy (or cowgirl) in your life.

Finished Measurements: One finished quilt block measures 5-1/2 x 5-1/2 inches (minus seam allowance); finished quilt measures 11 blocks wide and 13 blocks long, or 66 x 75-1/2 inches with added borders (minus edging).

Cut the number of pieces of each color as indicated on the pattern. Start machine or hand stitching the quilt block pieces, according to the diagram. Make all 143 quilt blocks in the same manner.

Stitch blocks together by rows. Pin corners first, followed by the seams, then stitch with short running stitches. Join finished rows two at a time, matching vertical seams before sewing. Add borders as directed.

Finishing: Quilt stitch or tie. Then add desired binding to edges of completed quilt.

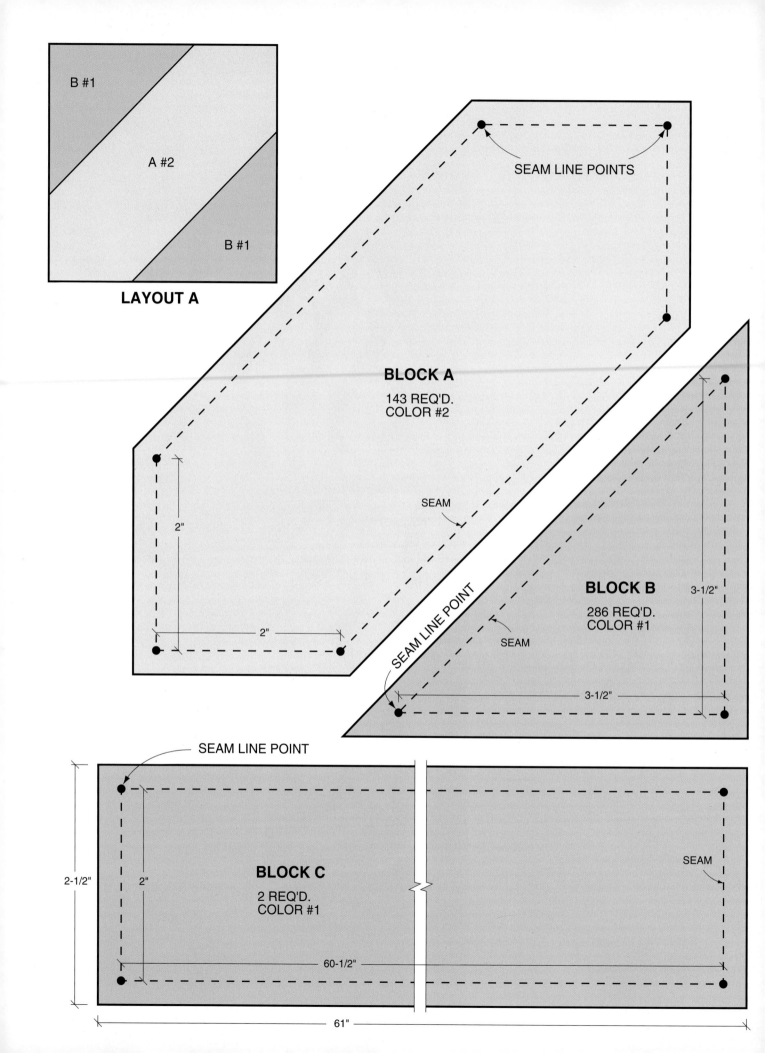

B #1

A #2

B #1

LAYOUT A

SEAM LINE POINTS

BLOCK A

143 REQ'D.
COLOR #2

SEAM

2"

2"

SEAM LINE POINT

BLOCK B

286 REQ'D.
COLOR #1

SEAM

3-1/2"

3-1/2"

SEAM LINE POINT

BLOCK C

2 REQ'D.
COLOR #1

SEAM

2-1/2"

2"

60-1/2"

61"

C

D

D

C

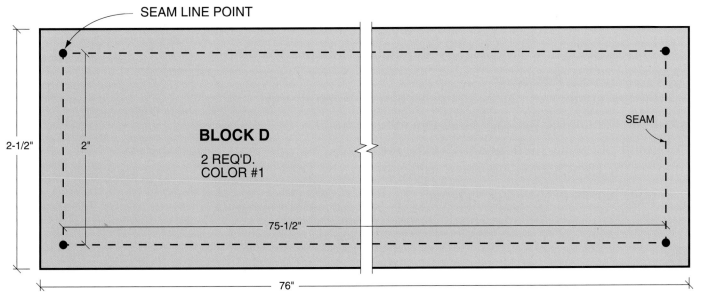

SEAM LINE POINT

BLOCK D

2 REQ'D.
COLOR #1

2-1/2"

2"

75-1/2"

76"

SEAM

Geese In Flight

Using Nine Patch construction, this easy quilt block pattern draws symbolism from nature. American settlers and westward bound pioneers were closely in tune to their surroundings. Therefore, it is not surprising that their quilt designs were derivative of animals and plants. Perhaps birds and geese were particular favorites because they embody both freedom and movement, traits common to the pioneer spirit.

LAYOUT A

Finished Measurements: One finished quilt block measures 9 x 9 inches (minus seam allowance); the finished quilt measures six blocks wide and six blocks long, or 77 x 77 inches with added sashing and borders (minus edging).

Cut the number of pieces of each color as indicated on the pattern. Start machine or hand stitching quilt block pieces. following the step-by-step diagrams. Make all 36 quilt blocks in the same manner.

Stitch the blocks together by rows, adding a strip of sashing between pieced blocks. Pin corners first, followed by seams, then stitch with short running stitches. Likewise, stitch together five full rows of sashing. Join each finished row of blocks with a row of sashing. (One row of blocks will be without sashing. This row will be the bottom row, when finished.) Join the resulting rows two at a time, matching vertical seams before sewing. Add borders to quilt edges.

Finishing: Quilt stitch or tie. Then, add desired binding to edges of completed quilt.

SEAM LINE POINT

SEAM

BLOCK B

324 REQ'D.
COLOR #1

324 REQ'D.
COLOR #2

3"

3"

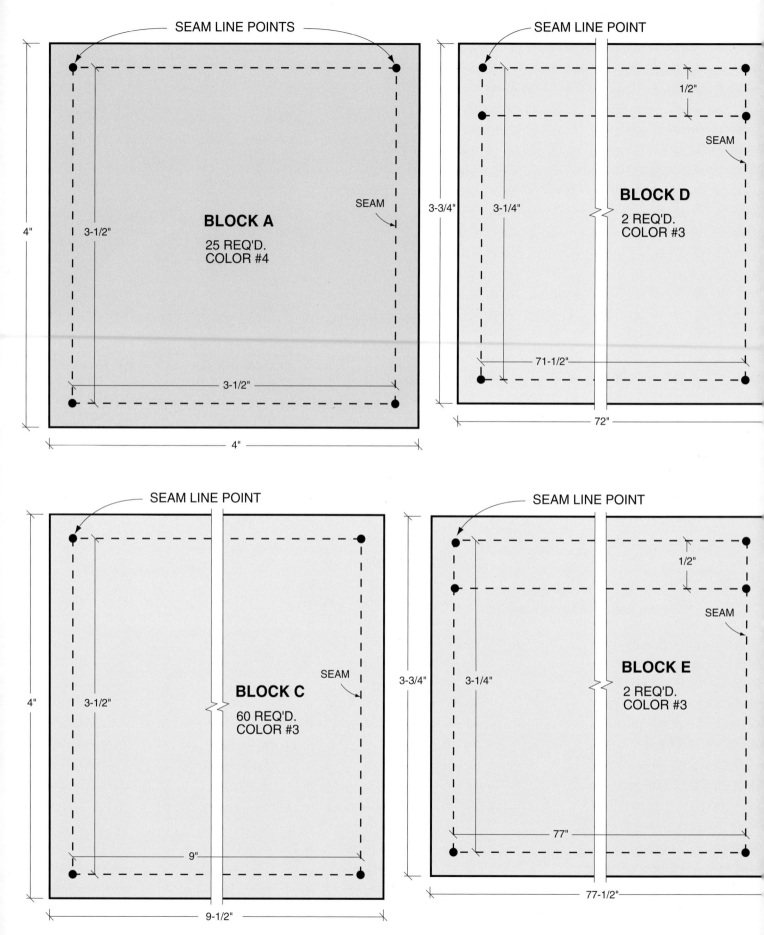

SEAM LINE POINTS

BLOCK A

25 REQ'D.
COLOR #4

4"

3-1/2"

SEAM

3-1/2"

4"

SEAM LINE POINT

BLOCK D

2 REQ'D.
COLOR #3

1/2"

SEAM

3-3/4"

3-1/4"

71-1/2"

72"

SEAM LINE POINT

BLOCK C

60 REQ'D.
COLOR #3

4"

3-1/2"

SEAM

9"

9-1/2"

SEAM LINE POINT

BLOCK E

2 REQ'D.
COLOR #3

1/2"

SEAM

3-3/4"

3-1/4"

77"

77-1/2"

110

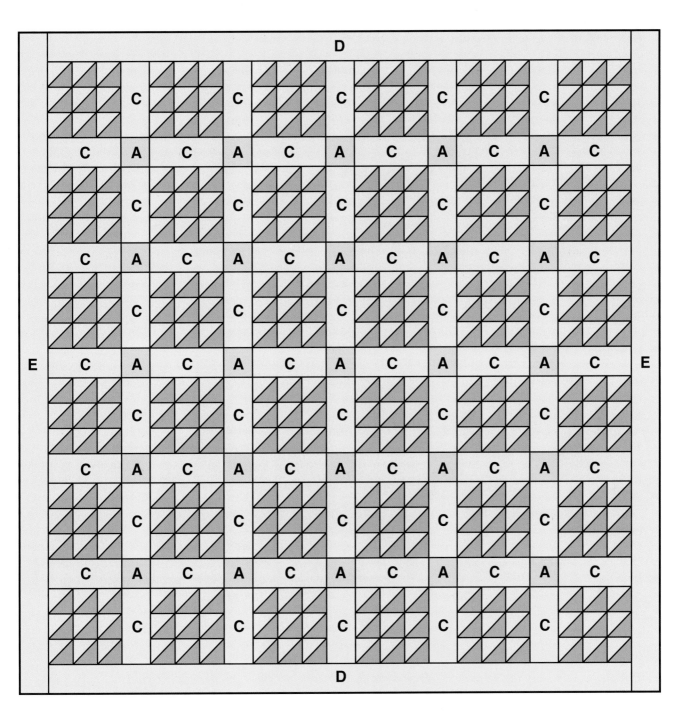

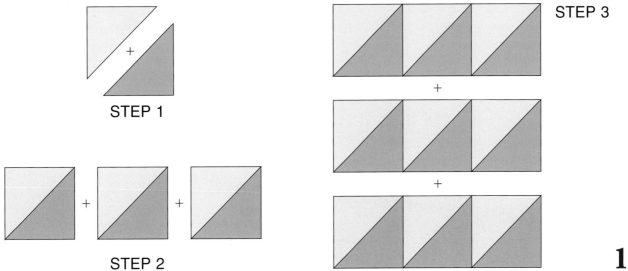

STEP 1

STEP 2

STEP 3

111

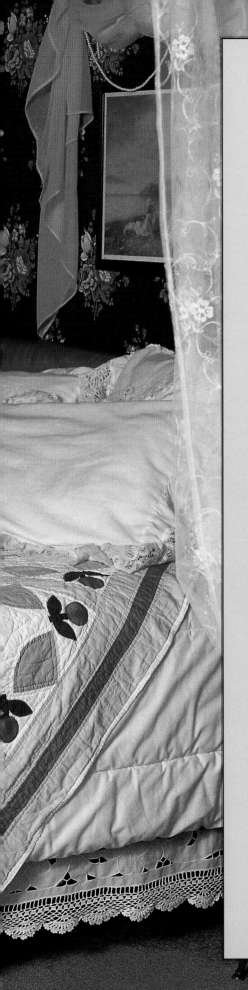

Cherry Blossom

This unique quilt block pattern is actually the successful blending of two heirloom patterns. It takes a design from a traditionally-pieced block and incorporates it with a familiar appliqué motif.

The central block, otherwise known as The Mill Wheel, is handled as an appliqué and then is turned on the diagonal. Triangles are appliquéed with a classic Love Apple motif from the mid-19th century. These triangles are then added to the center block, creating the Cherry Blossom quilt pattern.

Finished Measurements: One finished quilt block measures 12 x 12 inches (minus seam allowance); the finished quilt shown in photo measures four blocks wide and five blocks long, or 64-1/2 x 78-1/2 inches with sashing and borders added (minus edging).

Cut the number of pieces of each color as indicated on the pattern. Start machine or hand appliquéing and assembling pieces, following the step-by-step diagrams. Make all 20 quilt blocks in the same manner.

Stitch the blocks together by rows, adding sashing pieces between blocks. Prepare four complete rows of sashing. Pin corners first, followed by seams, then stitch with short running stitches. Stitch one row of sashing to one row of blocks, then join these rows two at a time. Be sure to match vertical seams before sewing. Add borders as shown in quilt layout.

Finishing: Quilt stitch or tie. Then, add desired binding to edges of completed quilt.

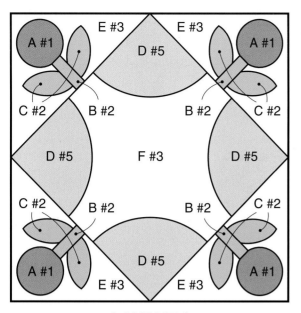

LAYOUT A

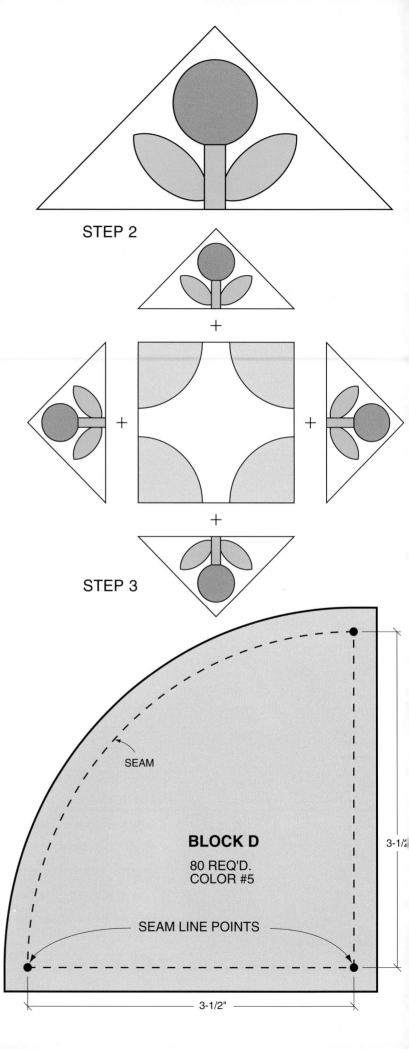

STEP 2

+

+ +

+

STEP 3

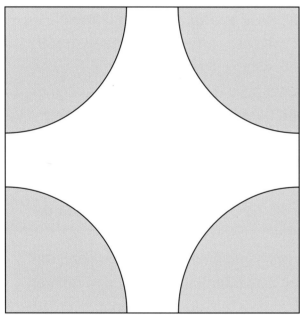

STEP 1

SEAM LINE
POINT

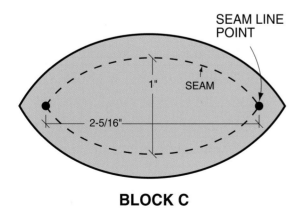

1"

SEAM

2-5/16"

BLOCK C

160 REQ'D.
COLOR #2

BLOCK D

80 REQ'D.
COLOR #5

SEAM

SEAM LINE POINTS

3-1/2"

3-1/2"

114

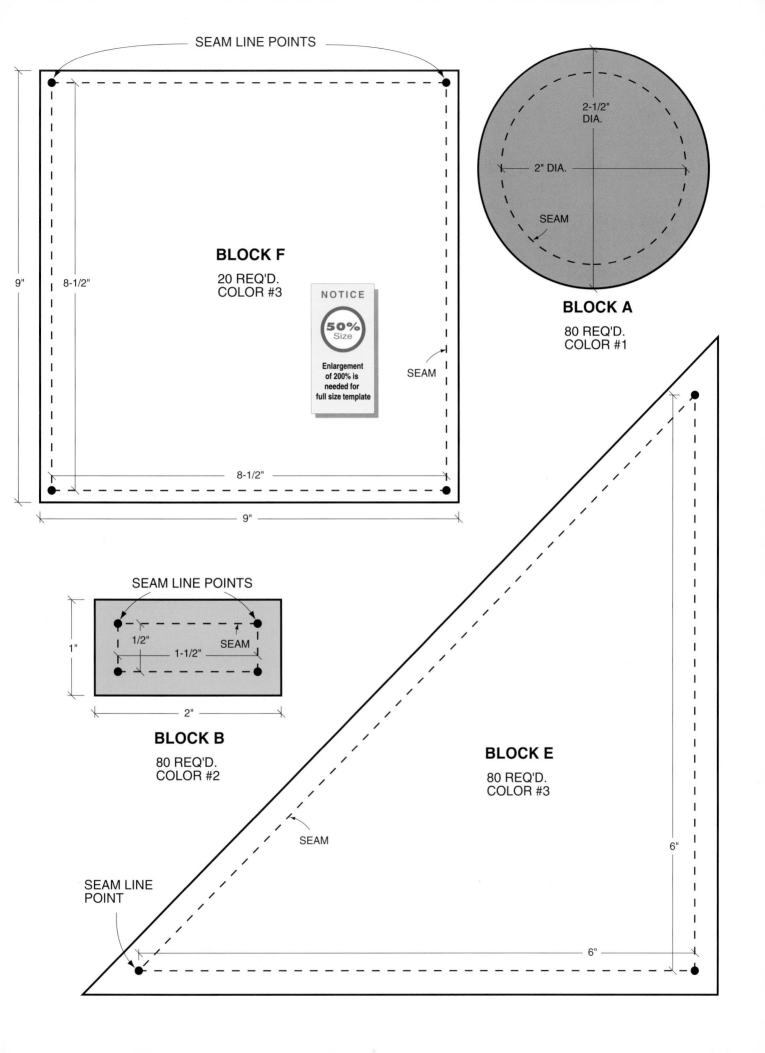

SEAM LINE POINTS

BLOCK F

20 REQ'D.
COLOR #3

NOTICE

50% Size

Enlargement of 200% is needed for full size template

SEAM

9"

8-1/2"

8-1/2"

9"

2-1/2" DIA.

2" DIA.

SEAM

BLOCK A

80 REQ'D.
COLOR #1

SEAM LINE POINTS

1/2"

SEAM

1-1/2"

1"

2"

BLOCK B

80 REQ'D.
COLOR #2

SEAM

BLOCK E

80 REQ'D.
COLOR #3

SEAM LINE POINT

6"

6"

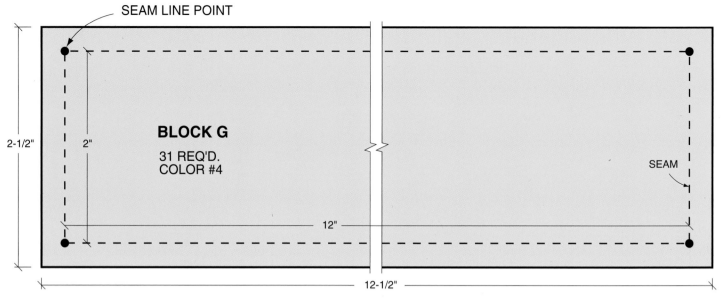

SEAM LINE POINT

BLOCK G

31 REQ'D.
COLOR #4

2-1/2"

2"

12"

SEAM

12-1/2"

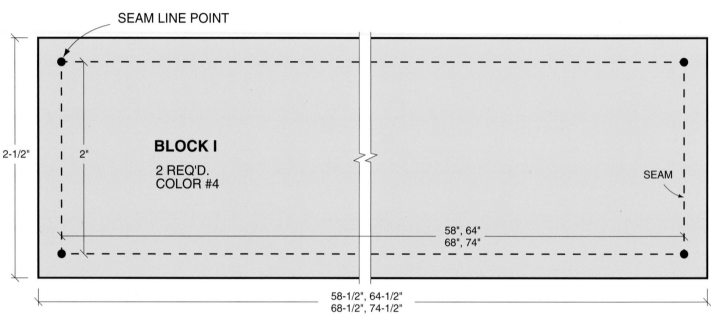

SEAM LINE POINT

BLOCK I

2 REQ'D.
COLOR #4

2-1/2"

2"

58", 64"
68", 74"

SEAM

58-1/2", 64-1/2"
68-1/2", 74-1/2"

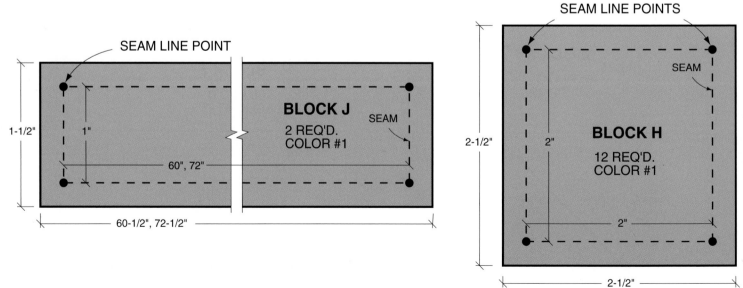

SEAM LINE POINT

BLOCK J

2 REQ'D.
COLOR #1

1-1/2"

1"

60", 72"

SEAM

60-1/2", 72-1/2"

SEAM LINE POINTS

BLOCK H

12 REQ'D.
COLOR #1

2-1/2"

2"

SEAM

2"

2-1/2"

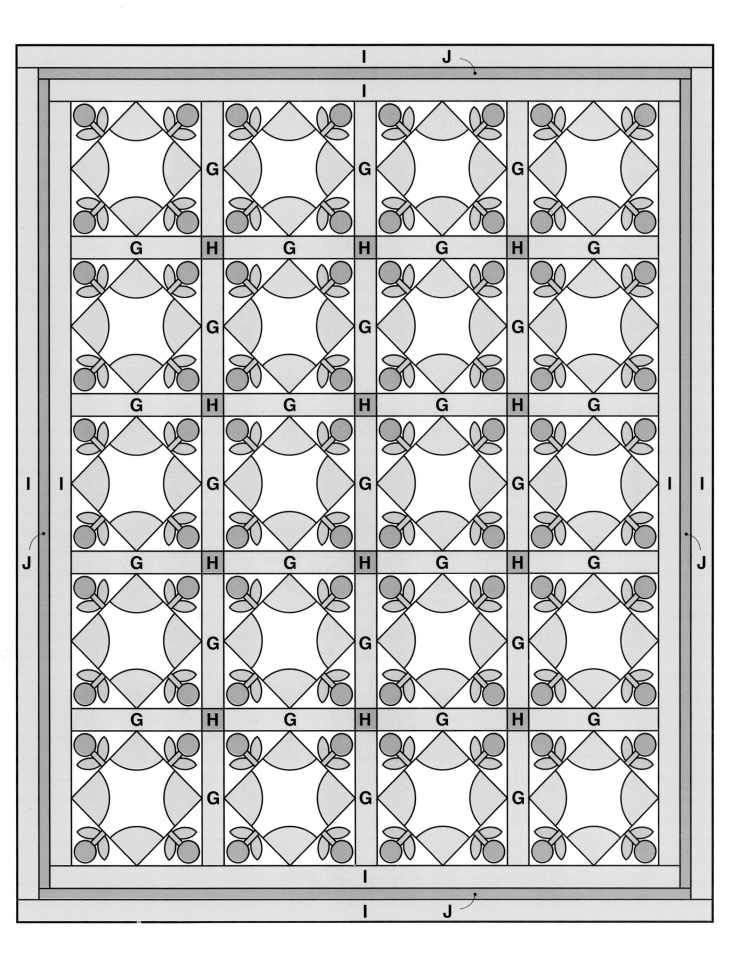

Arkansas Finds

Often referred to as a mosaic or honeycomb pattern, this type of design was popular in America between 1880 and 1900. However, the hexagon one-patch has been a staple of English quilting for more than 200 years. Researchers believe this pattern favorite may have been inspired by ancient Mediterranean tiles and mosaics.

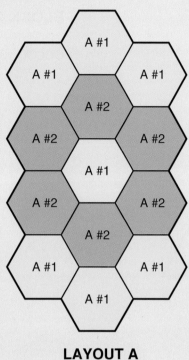

LAYOUT A

The Arkansas Finds design is distinguished from other hexagonal designs by its color choices and placements. Pieced to form a mass of blossoms, one would imagine that the original designer visited Arkansas during the springtime bloom and was inspired.

Finished Measurements: The pictured quilt is based on a single hexagon piece, which measures 1-5/8 inches across at the widest point. The finished quilt, with 3-inch borders, measures approximately 70 x 84 inches (minus edging).

Cut the number of pieces of each color as indicated on the pattern. Start machine or hand stitching, matching seam points for accuracy. Follow the step-by-step diagrams to piece flower blocks, making 143 in the same manner. Stitch the blocks together, filling in with blue hexagons to complete the layout. Match seam points, then stitch with short running stitches.

Add borders if desired.

Finishing: Quilt stitch or tie. Then, add desired binding to the edges of completed quilt.

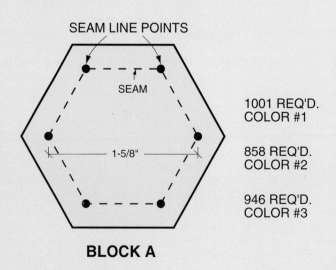

BLOCK A

SEAM LINE POINTS

SEAM

1-5/8"

1001 REQ'D. COLOR #1

858 REQ'D. COLOR #2

946 REQ'D. COLOR #3

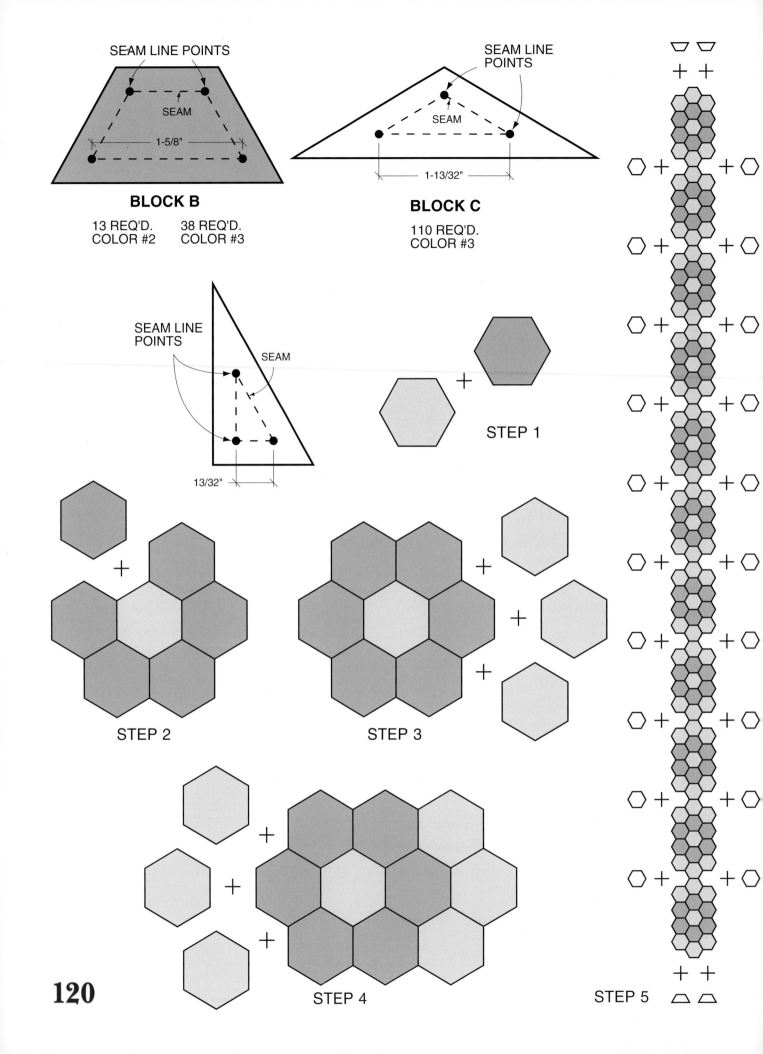

SEAM LINE POINTS

SEAM

1-5/8"

BLOCK B

13 REQ'D.
COLOR #2

38 REQ'D.
COLOR #3

SEAM LINE POINTS

SEAM

1-13/32"

BLOCK C

110 REQ'D.
COLOR #3

SEAM LINE POINTS

SEAM

13/32"

STEP 1

STEP 2

STEP 3

STEP 4

STEP 5

120

C #1	C #2	B #1			C #2	C #1
C #2	C #1	C #2	C #1	C #2	C #1	C #2
	C #2	C #1	C #2	C #1	C #2	
B #1	C #1	C #2	C #1	C #2	C #1	B #1
	C #2	C #1	C #2	C #1	C #2	
C #2	C #1	C #2	C #1	C #2	C #1	C #2
C #1	C #2	B #1			C #2	C #1

122   **LAYOUT A**

STEP 1

Double Irish Chain

This easy quilt block pattern is a variation of the "Irish chain," which dates back to the early 19th century. The assembly is merely an extension of the methods used in simple Four Patch and Nine Patch patterns. Relying completely on straight seams, piecing this heirloom quilt is a pleasure.

Early Irish Chain quilts were often used to showcase fancy embroidery. The blocks with a plain center served as picture frames for elaborate embroideries and Broderie Perse appliqués. At the very least, this space was a blank canvas for decorative quilt stitch designs.

Finished Measurements: One finished quilt block will measure 14 x 14 inches (minus seam allowance); the finished quilt measures five blocks wide and five blocks long, or 70-1/2 x 76-1/2 inches after borders are added (minus edging).

Cut the number of pieces of each color as indicated on the pattern. Start machine or hand stitching the quilt block pieces, following the step-by-step diagrams. Make 13 Type A quilt blocks and 12 Type B quilt blocks.

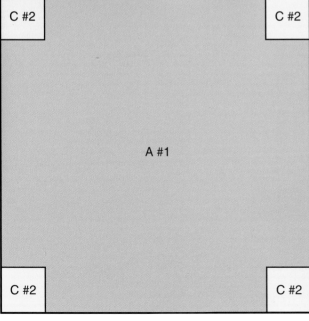

C #2   C #2

A #1

C #2   C #2

LAYOUT B

123

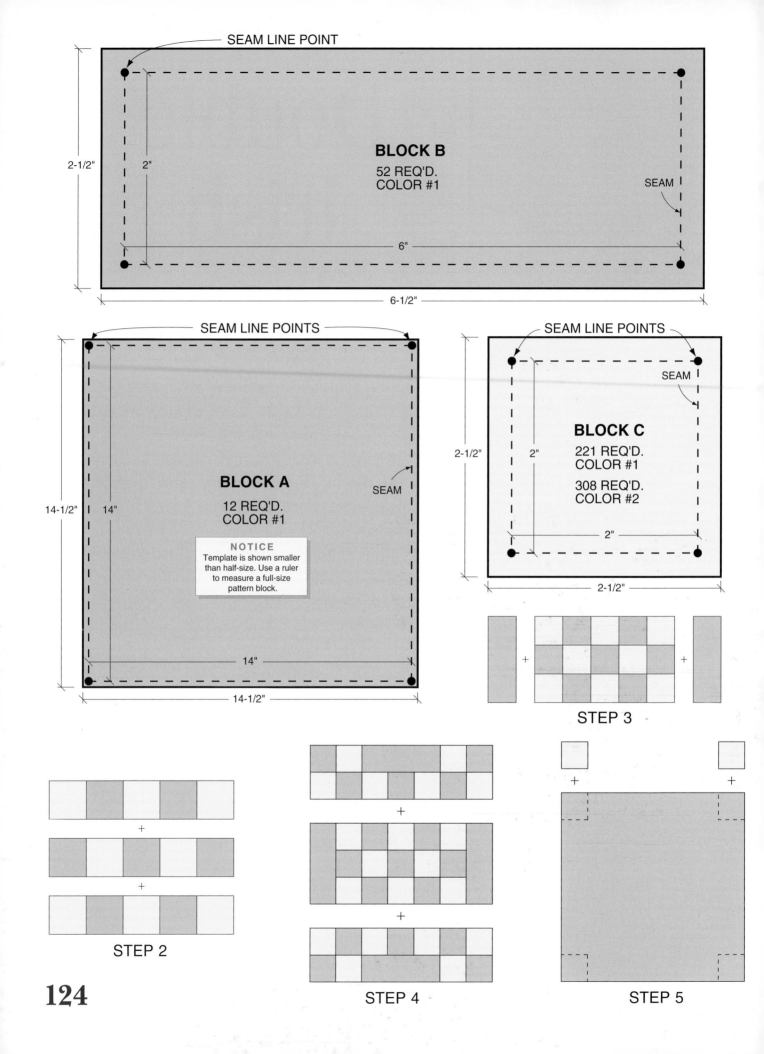

SEAM LINE POINT

BLOCK B
52 REQ'D.
COLOR #1

2-1/2"

2"

SEAM

6"

6-1/2"

SEAM LINE POINTS

SEAM

BLOCK A
12 REQ'D.
COLOR #1

NOTICE
Template is shown smaller
than half-size. Use a ruler
to measure a full-size
pattern block.

14-1/2"

14"

14"

14-1/2"

SEAM LINE POINTS

SEAM

BLOCK C
221 REQ'D.
COLOR #1

308 REQ'D.
COLOR #2

2-1/2"

2"

2"

2-1/2"

+   +

STEP 3

+

+

STEP 2

+

+

STEP 4

+   +

STEP 5

124

Stitch the blocks together by rows, alternating Type A and B blocks according to quilt layout. Begin three rows with Type A blocks and two rows with Type B blocks. Pin corners first, followed by the seams, then stitch with short running stitches.

Join finished rows two at a time, matching vertical seams before sewing. Add borders to top and bottom of quilt top.

Finishing: Quilt stitch or tie. Then, add desired binding to edges of completed quilt.

Twinkle Star

The star, a universal and easily recognizable symbol, is among the most popular element found in quilt block patterns. Based on an octagon, the eight-pointed star has likewise been among the most favorite of the star block designs.

Unlike most eight-pointed stars, however, the stars in this pattern are applied to plain squares as appliqués rather than pieced. With the addition of the diamond border, this quilt will surely add a twinkle to a loved one's eye.

Finished Measurements: One finished quilt block measures 4 x 4 inches (minus seam allowance); finished quilt measures 10 blocks wide and 16 blocks long, or 62-1/4 x 88-1/2 inches with added borders (minus edging),

Cut the number of pieces of each color as indicated on the pattern. Start machine or hand stitching quilt block pieces, following the step-by-step diagrams. Make 80 quilt blocks in the same manner.

Stitch the blocks together by rows, alternating a star block with a plain block. Pin corners first, followed by the seams, then stitch with short running stitches. Join finished rows two at a time, reversing rows so that every other row begins with a plain block. Match vertical seams before sewing.

Prepare diamond border as shown in diagram. Then, attach the diamond border followed by the 10-inch border.

Finishing: Quilt stitch or tie. Then, add desired binding to edges of completed quilt.

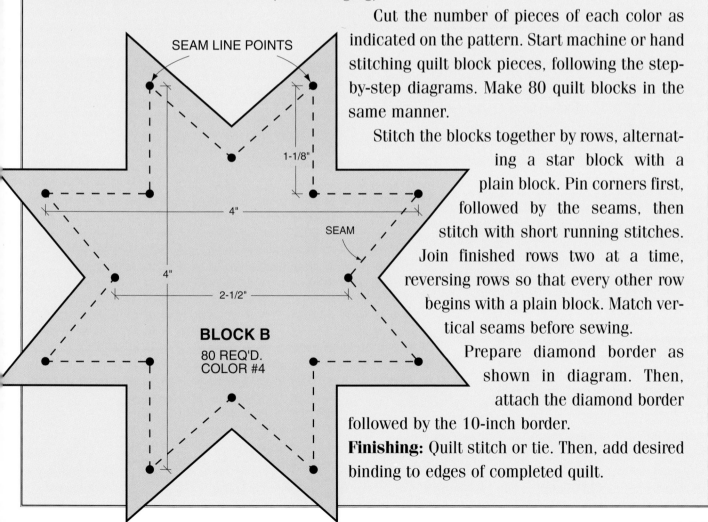

SEAM LINE POINTS

1-1/8"

4"

SEAM

4"

2-1/2"

BLOCK B
80 REQ'D.
COLOR #4

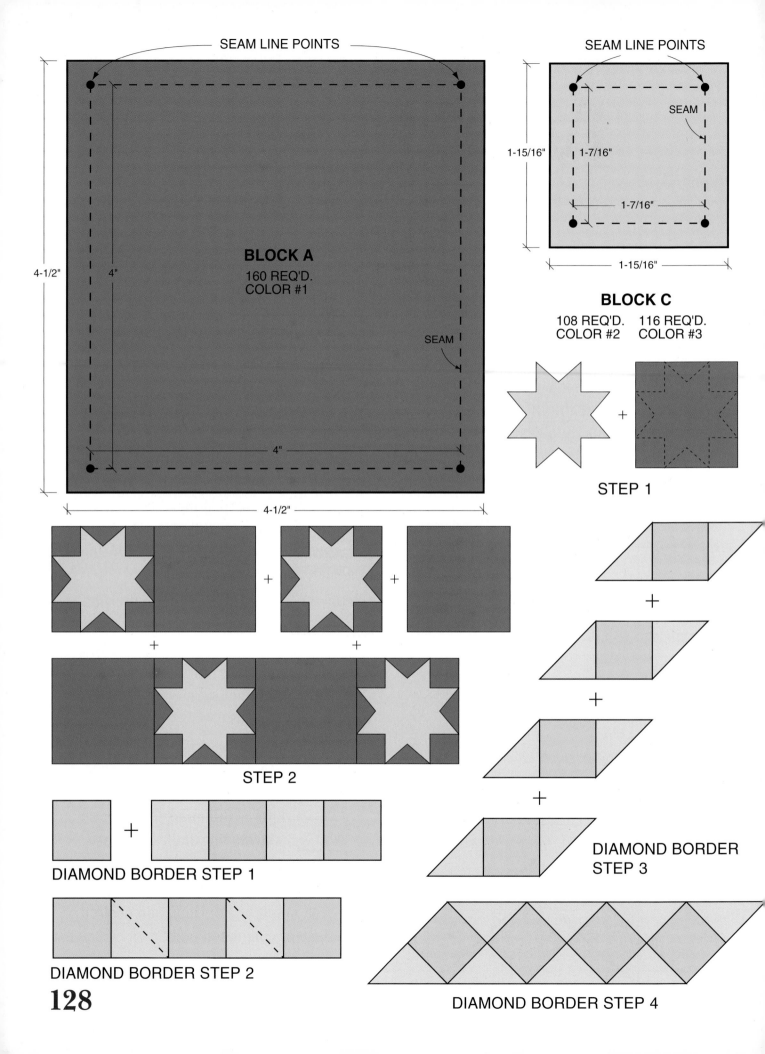

SEAM LINE POINTS

BLOCK A
160 REQ'D.
COLOR #1

4-1/2"

4"

4"

4"

4-1/2"

SEAM

SEAM LINE POINTS

1-15/16"

1-7/16"

1-7/16"

SEAM

1-15/16"

BLOCK C
108 REQ'D.   116 REQ'D.
COLOR #2   COLOR #3

+

STEP 1

+

+

STEP 2

+

+

+

DIAMOND BORDER
STEP 3

DIAMOND BORDER STEP 1

+

DIAMOND BORDER STEP 2

DIAMOND BORDER STEP 4

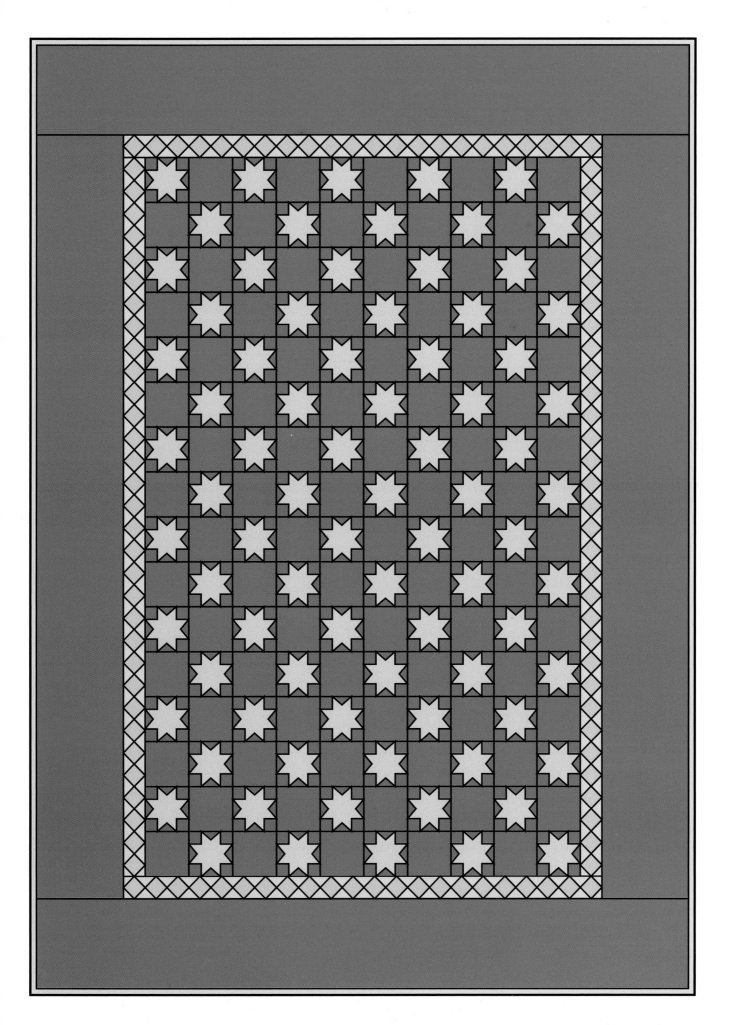

Jacob's Ladder

Comprised of both Four Patch and Nine Patch elements, this pattern has many adaptations and carries many various names. The slightest alteration of the diamond blocks or rearrangement of fabric placement can bring surprising results. Often, close scrutiny is necessary to recognize a related pattern, since the appearance is so easily altered.

Some variations include: The Broken Bowl, Double Hour Glass, The Railroad, Trail of the Covered Wagon, and Tail of Benjamin's Kite. Since Jacob's Ladder was a favorite quilt pattern both to make and to alter, there are undoubtedly many more names and variations never recorded.

Finished Measurements: One finished quilt block measures 9 x 9 inches (minus seam allowance); finished quilt measures five blocks wide and six blocks long (diagonally set), or 68-1/4 x 82 inches with borders added (minus edging).

Cut the number of pieces of each color as indicated on the pattern. Start machine or hand stitching the quilt block pieces, according to the step-by-step diagrams. Make all 30 quilt blocks in the same manner.

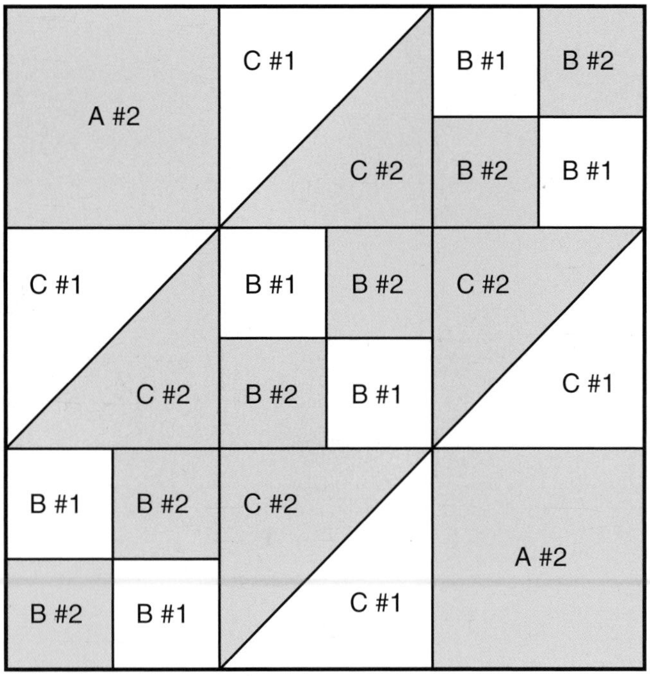
A #2
C #1
C #2
B #1
B #2
B #2
B #1
C #1
B #1
B #2
C #2
C #2
B #2
B #1
C #1
B #1
B #2
C #2
A #2
B #2
B #1
C #1

LAYOUT A

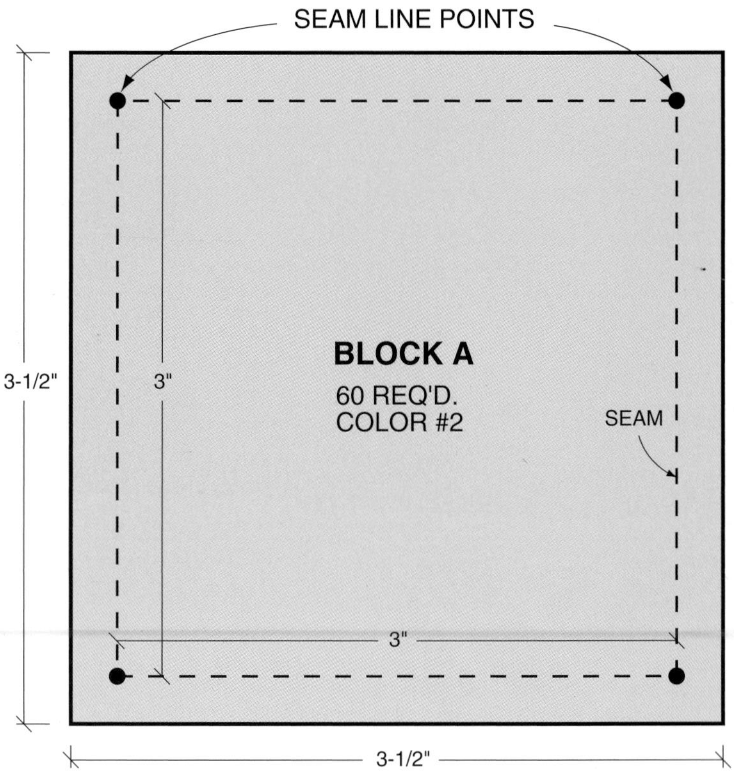
SEAM LINE POINTS
3-1/2"
3"
BLOCK A
60 REQ'D.
COLOR #2
SEAM
3"
3-1/2"

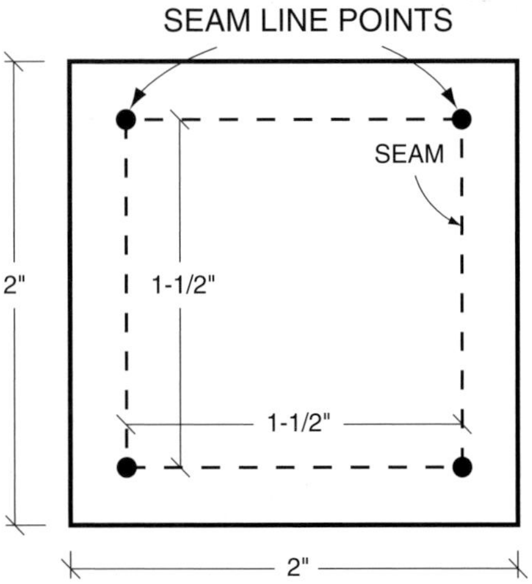
SEAM LINE POINTS
SEAM
2"
1-1/2"
1-1/2"
2"

BLOCK B

180 REQ'D.
COLOR #1

180 REQ'D.
COLOR #2

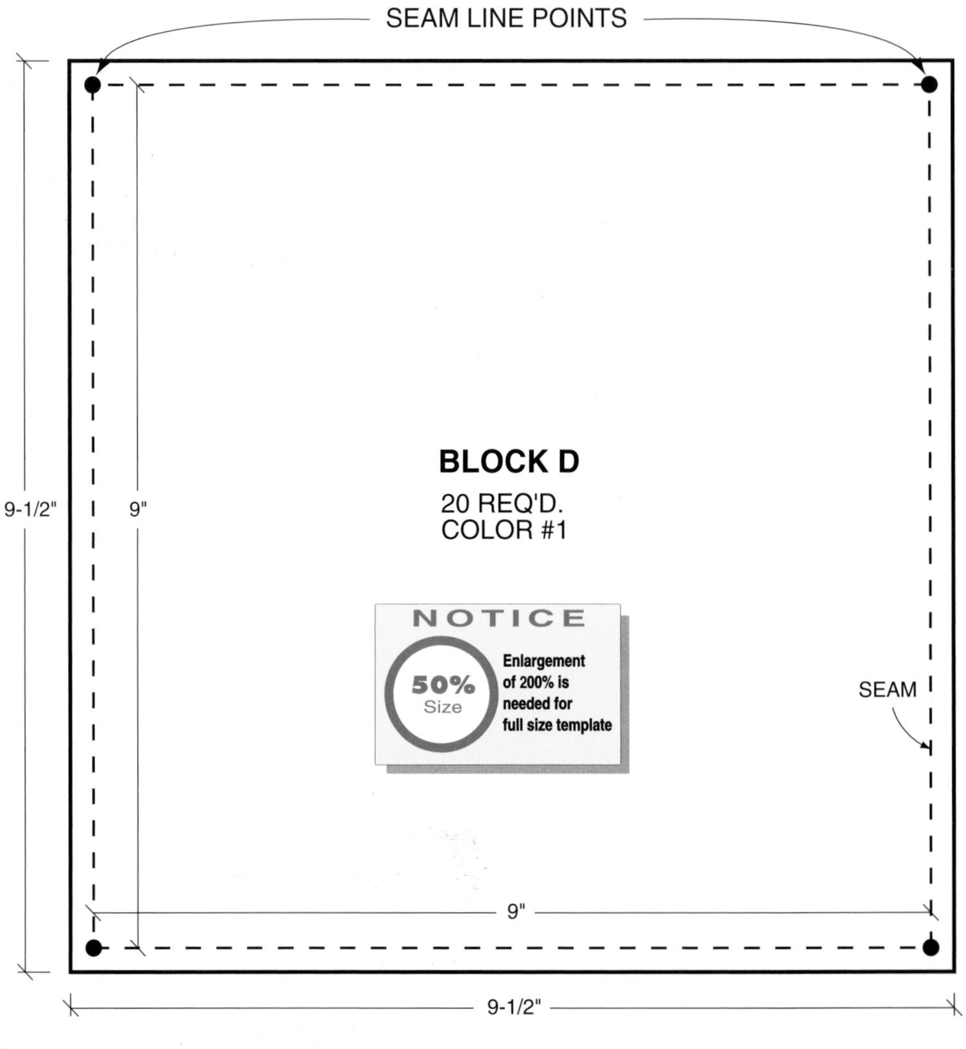
SEAM LINE POINTS
9-1/2"
9"
BLOCK D
20 REQ'D.
COLOR #1
NOTICE
50% Size
Enlargement of 200% is needed for full size template
SEAM
9"
9-1/2"

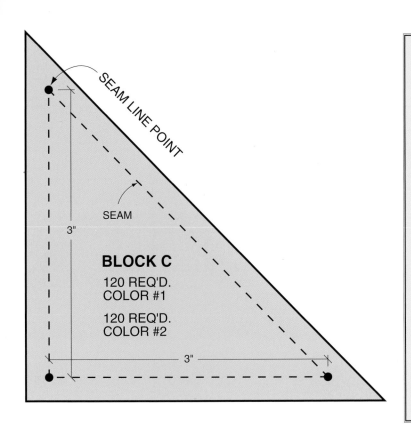

BLOCK C

120 REQ'D.
COLOR #1

120 REQ'D.
COLOR #2

SEAM LINE POINT

SEAM

3"

3"

Stitch the blocks together by rows, alternating pieced squares with plain and adding partial pieces as shown. Pin corners first, followed by seams, then stitch with short running stitches. Join finished rows two at a time, being sure to match intersecting seams before stitching. Add borders to quilt top.

Finishing: Quilt stitch or tie according to preference. Then bind edges of completed quilt.

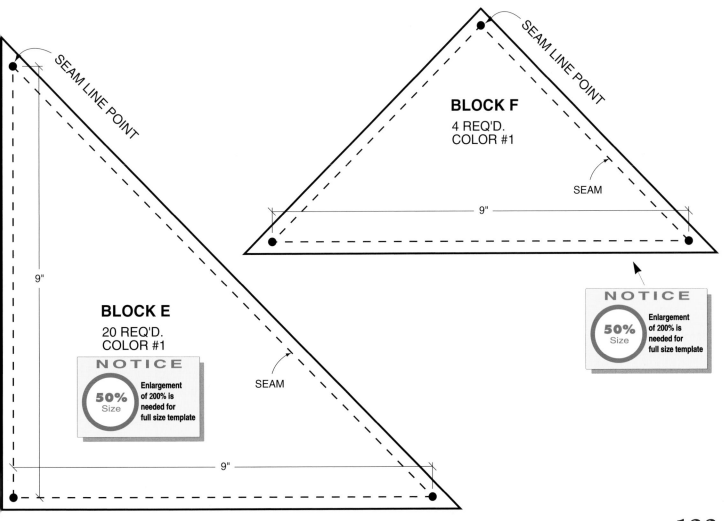

BLOCK E

20 REQ'D.
COLOR #1

SEAM LINE POINT

SEAM

9"

9"

NOTICE

50% Size

Enlargement of 200% is needed for full size template

BLOCK F

4 REQ'D.
COLOR #1

SEAM LINE POINT

SEAM

9"

NOTICE

50% Size

Enlargement of 200% is needed for full size template

133

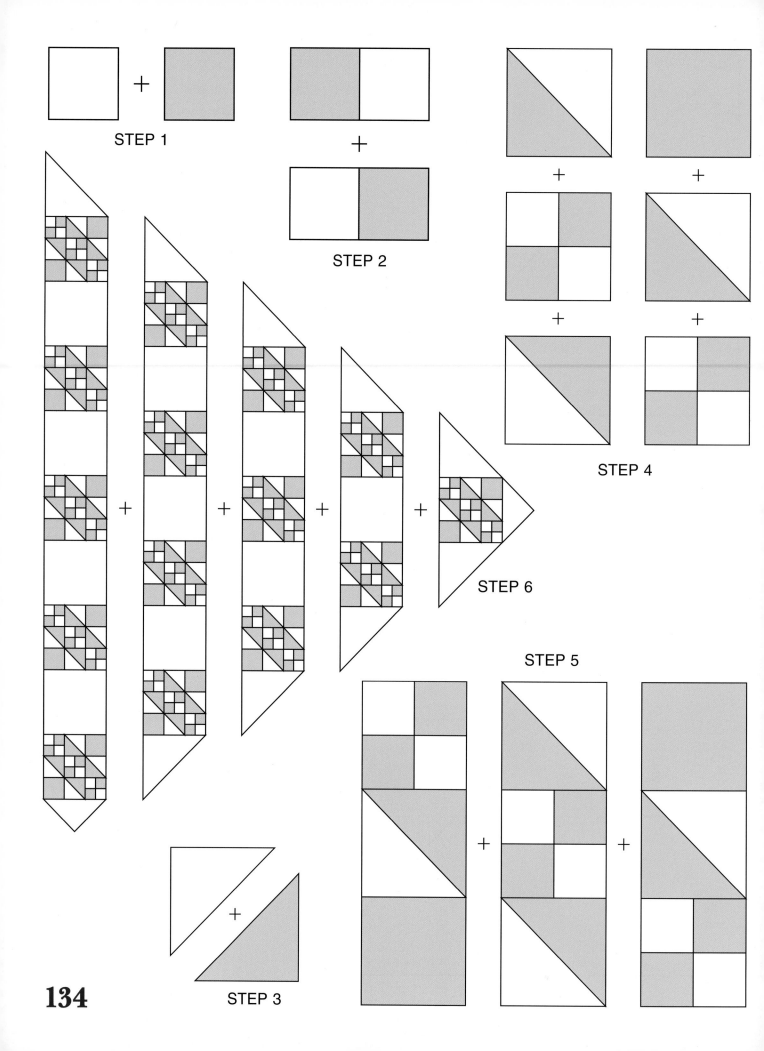

STEP 1

STEP 2

STEP 3

STEP 4

STEP 5

STEP 6

134

F #1   E #1   E #1   E #1   E #1   F #1

E #1   D #1   D #1   D #1   D #1   E #1

E #1   D #1   D #1   D #1   D #1   E #1

E #1   D #1   D #1   D #1   D #1   E #1

E #1   D #1   D #1   D #1   D #1   E #1

E #1   D #1   D #1   D #1   D #1   E #1

F #1   E #1   E #1   E #1   E #1   F #1

Dresden Plate
With Ice Cream Cone Border

This pattern combines both pieced and appliqué techniques. First, flowers are pieced, stitching petals together side-by-side. The flower is then centered on the foundation block, and applied as one large appliqué.

Often used as a friendship quilt, the Dresden Plate design requires quite a large cache of fabric scraps. Each flower consists of 20 petals, a different small print for each petal. Sharing scraps among friends would, therefore, be beneficial.

Finished Measurements: One finished quilt block measures 15 x 15 inches (minus seam allowance); the finished quilt measures four blocks wide and five blocks long, or 68-1/2 x 83-1/2 inches with border (minus edging).

Cut the number of pieces of each color as indicated on the pattern. Start machine or hand piecing the petal pieces, following the step-by-

step diagrams. Long, straight edges of petals are joined to form a whole flower. Next, turn the 1/4-inch seam allowance under all around the curved edges of the petals. Press and baste, if necessary. Then, apply the flower as an appliqué. Center the flower on the foundation block and blind stitch it into place. The inside circle (Block B) of the flower must also be turned under 1/4 inch and pressed; clip within the seam allowance as necessary for a smooth curve. Center this piece in the middle of the flower appliqué, as shown in the step-by-step diagrams. Be sure to cover the raw inside edges of the petals with this center piece and blind stitch into place. Make all 20 quilt blocks in the same manner.

Stitch the blocks together in rows. Pin corners first, followed by the seams, then stitch with short running stitches. Join finished rows two at a time, matching vertical seams before

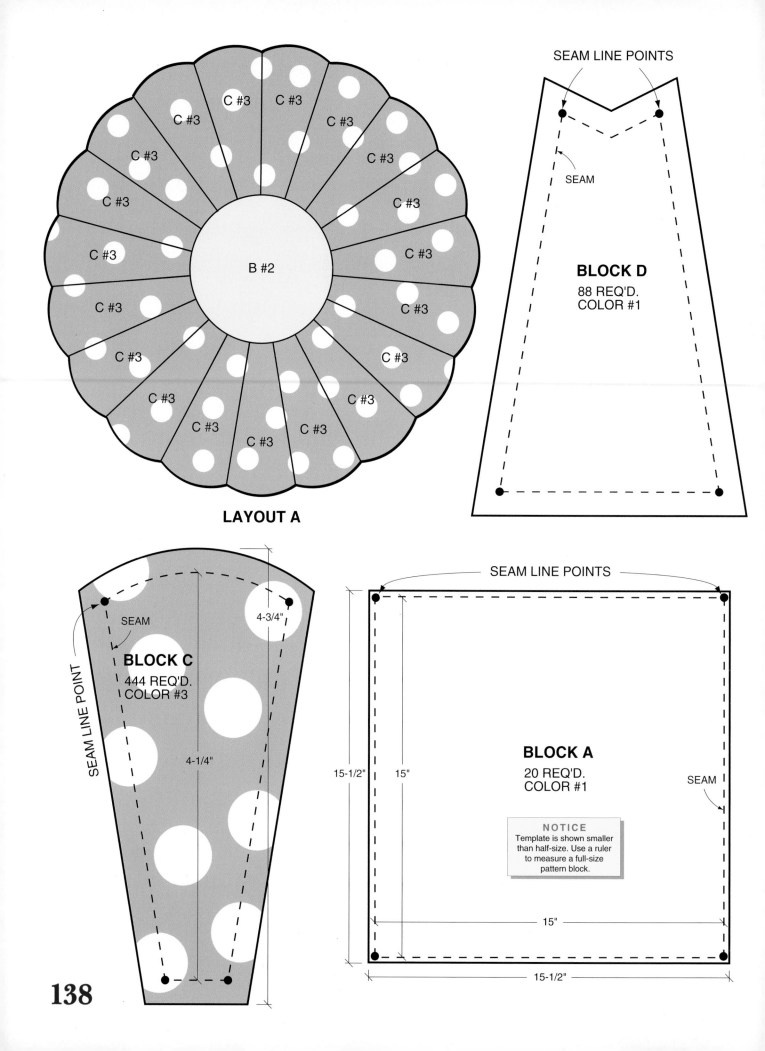

SEAM LINE POINTS

BLOCK D
88 REQ'D.
COLOR #1

SEAM

LAYOUT A

C #3
B #2

4-3/4"

SEAM

SEAM LINE POINT

BLOCK C
444 REQ'D.
COLOR #3

4-1/4"

SEAM LINE POINTS

BLOCK A
20 REQ'D.
COLOR #1

15-1/2"

15"

SEAM

15"

15-1/2"

NOTICE
Template is shown smaller
than half-size. Use a ruler
to measure a full-size
pattern block.

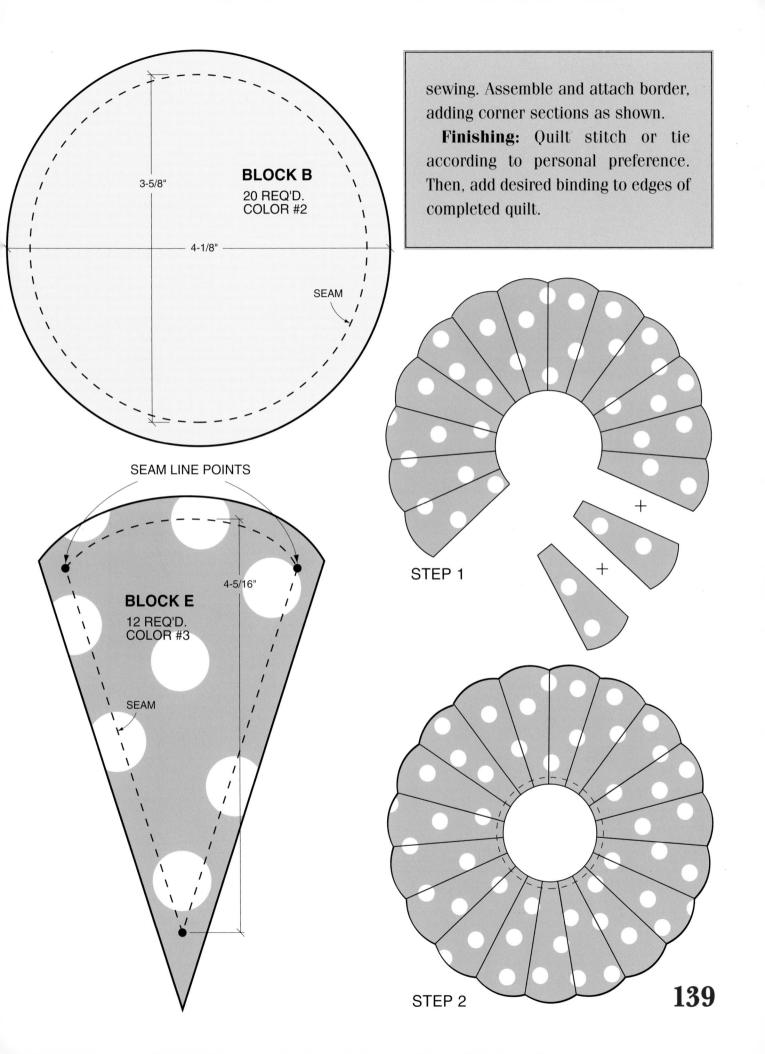

BLOCK B
20 REQ'D.
COLOR #2

3-5/8"

4-1/8"

SEAM

SEAM LINE POINTS

BLOCK E
12 REQ'D.
COLOR #3

4-5/16"

SEAM

sewing. Assemble and attach border, adding corner sections as shown.

Finishing: Quilt stitch or tie according to personal preference. Then, add desired binding to edges of completed quilt.

STEP 1

STEP 2

139

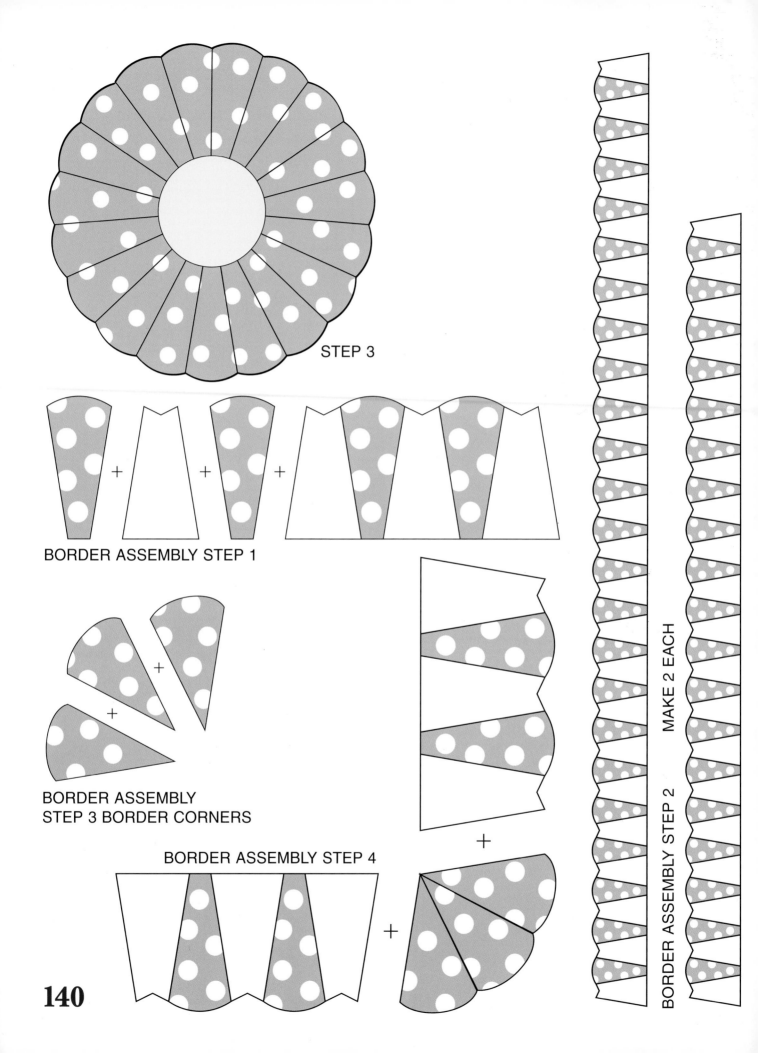

STEP 3

BORDER ASSEMBLY STEP 1

BORDER ASSEMBLY
STEP 3 BORDER CORNERS

BORDER ASSEMBLY STEP 4

MAKE 2 EACH

BORDER ASSEMBLY STEP 2

140

141

Tulip Quilt

Though examples of this pattern were popular during the 1840s, the pattern is based on a much older design. The Le Moyne Star pattern is named after French voyageurs who explored the Mississippi and founded New Orleans in 1718. All of the lily and tulip quilt patterns are based on this star.

This pattern, as shown here, is like those found among patterns of the early 19th century. Assembled with both pieced and appliqué techniques, the quilt has been known both as Peony and as Tulip. With either name, the completed quilt turns any ordinary bed into a bed of blooming flowers.

Finished Measurements: One finished quilt block measures 9 x 9 inches (minus seam allowance); finished quilt measures four blocks wide and six blocks long, plus sashing, or 58 x 85 inches (minus edging).

Cut the number of pieces of each color as indicated on the pattern. Start machine or hand stitching the quilt block pieces, following the step-by-step diagrams. Make all 24 quilt blocks in the same manner.

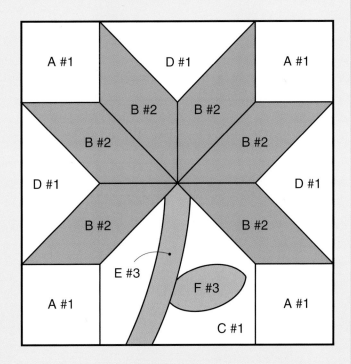

LAYOUT A

Stitch the blocks together by rows, adding stripping pieces between blocks. Prepare five complete rows of sashing and attach one to the bottom of each block row. Pin corners first, followed by the seams, then stitch with short running stitches. Join the resulting rows two at a time, matching vertical seams before sewing. Add borders to the edges of the quilt top.

Finishing: Quilt stitch or tie. Then add desired binding to the edges of completed quilt.

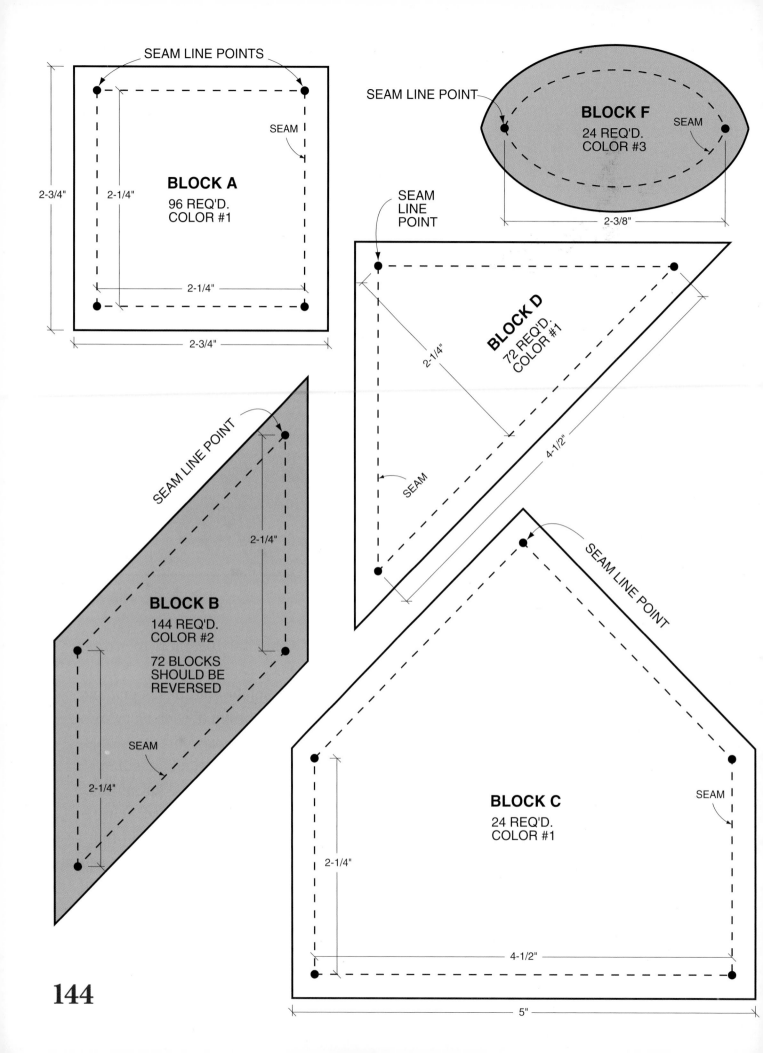

SEAM LINE POINTS

BLOCK A
96 REQ'D.
COLOR #1

2-3/4"
2-1/4"
2-1/4"
2-3/4"
SEAM

SEAM LINE POINT

BLOCK F
24 REQ'D.
COLOR #3

SEAM
2-3/8"

SEAM LINE POINT

BLOCK D
72 REQ'D.
COLOR #1

2-1/4"
4-1/2"
SEAM

SEAM LINE POINT

BLOCK B
144 REQ'D.
COLOR #2

72 BLOCKS
SHOULD BE
REVERSED

2-1/4"
2-1/4"
SEAM

SEAM LINE POINT

BLOCK C
24 REQ'D.
COLOR #1

2-1/4"
4-1/2"
5"
SEAM

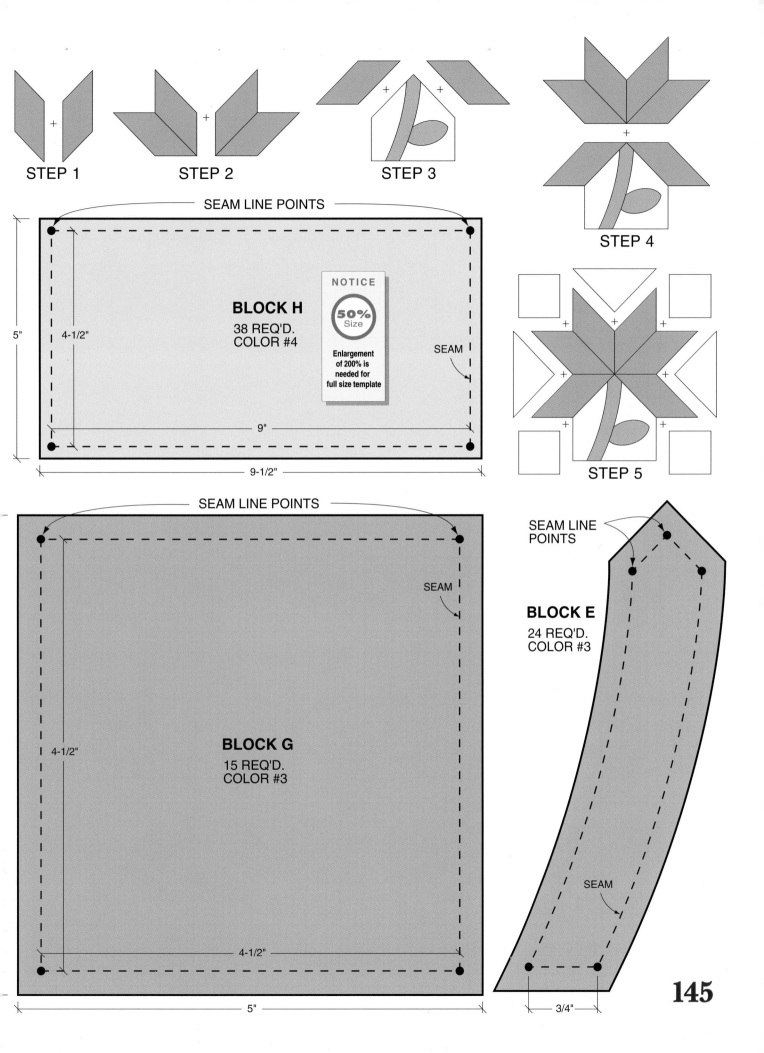

STEP 1

STEP 2

STEP 3

STEP 4

STEP 5

SEAM LINE POINTS

BLOCK H

38 REQ'D.
COLOR #4

NOTICE

50% Size

Enlargement
of 200% is
needed for
full size template

SEAM

5"

4-1/2"

9"

9-1/2"

SEAM LINE POINTS

SEAM

BLOCK G

15 REQ'D.
COLOR #3

4-1/2"

4-1/2"

5"

SEAM LINE
POINTS

BLOCK E

24 REQ'D.
COLOR #3

SEAM

3/4"

145

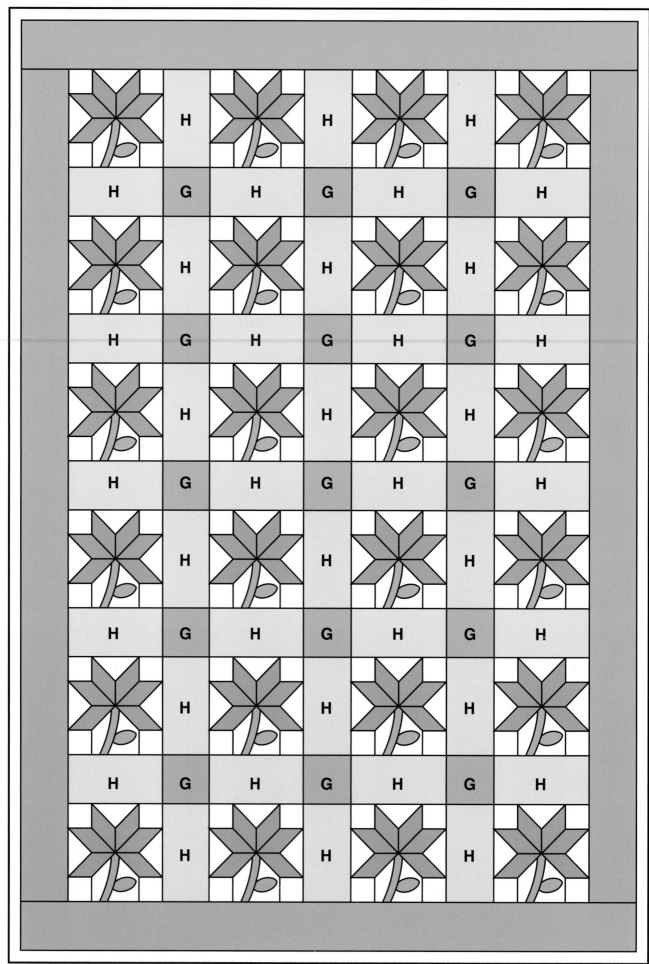

INDEX